A Red-shouldered Hawk

A RED-SHOULDERED HAWK

IN THE SWEET GUM TREE

SCRIPTURE IN VERSE

Second Edition

Charles R. Wilson

Published by Artisan House, Inc.
112 McCulloch, Eustis, FL 32726

Wilson, Charles R.

A Red-Shouldered Hawk in the Sweet Gum Tree

ISBN: 978-0990602712

Printed in the United States of America

Second Edition

Book Design by Artisan House

To The Glory of God
and in
Thanksgiving
for the
Wonder, Joy and Humor
of
Creating

We thank you for the splendor of the whole creation, for the beauty of this world, for the wonder of life, and for the mystery of love. And we thank you for setting us at tasks which demand our best efforts, and for leading us to accomplishments which satisfy and delight us.(BCP)

Table of Contents

In the Sweet Gum Tree

Blessed Lord, who has caused all holy scriptures to be written for our learning: Grant us so to hear them, read, mark, learn, and inwardly digest them, that we may embrace and ever hold fast the blessed hope of everlasting life, which you have given us in our Savior Jesus Christ; who lives and reigns with you and the Holy Spirit, one God, for ever and ever. Amen
    (BCP)

Glory to the Father, and to the Son, and to the Holy Spirit; as it was in the beginning, is now and will be forever, Amen.   Alleluia.

FOREWORD TO SECOND EDITION

To say that the publication of this book was my father's dying wish seems a trite way to phrase what was a passion for him right up to the end. But it was his final wish. Writing theological poetry had become Charles R. Wilson's greatest earthly joy, second only to the joy he experienced through his relationship with his God. When my father entered a hospital a couple of weeks ago, he thought it quite possible that his end had come. He was fine with that; he had lived a good life and death hath no fear for those whose love and life are based in God. His greatest concern was that this book be completed for family, friends and as his final statement to the world of his sense of fun, joy and reverence, all wrapped up in poetry.

Had he lived longer, this book would have continued growing. No concrete end to it exists as the joyful work kept flowing out of him, much faster than his editor (me!) could keep up. He asked me to choose a fitting ending poem from the new batch, and I believe I did, one which expresses clearly his love of God.

I will always remember him sitting at his desk, head turned to look out his sliding glass doors in deep thought and prayer at the lovely Florida landscape of lake and wetlands. He wanted very much to write a new foreword for the book but could not. Therefore, I wrote his new foreword as if it were him and he heartily approved it on the last day of his life. This is a gift to all of you, from my Dad, in love.

Charlene R. Johnson
Daughter & Editor

For Charles R. Wilson 6.13.1927 – 9.11.2015

In the Sweet Gum Tree

As I mentioned in the first edition of this book, I have continued to exercise poetic license. In the first book, I mentioned that it was fun putting it all together. But the joy I experienced while creating these poems has escalated far beyond fun. Over the last year since the first edition came out, and as I watched the Sweet Gum snag at the edge of the wetlands which is my backyard view gradually rot and finally fall, so that the pair of red-shouldered hawks who used to roost there were forced to find another good limb upon which to perch, so my sense of reverence for this amazing Creation we call Home and my Joy in the life I have led, increased. This book of poetry is my expression of this ever-growing Joy.

(Just as I sit here writing this, the female hawk soars down to land in the yard just outside my sliding glass doors, stretches her wings, then pounces upon some hapless prey!)

Approved by Charles R. Wilson

FOREWORD TO FIRST EDITION

Throughout this collection I have exercised poetic license with characters, history and Biblical literalism, but I have not knowingly sacrificed theological integrity. Getting it together has been fun. Some might recognize it as an exercise in Eolithic Creativity, which it is. See my earlier book on *Eolithic Homiletics* for more on that subject.

The short items in this collection might be suitable for greeting card use. For example, the first one, *LOGOS,* could be used as a Christmas card message. If you do this, I respectfully ask you to credit the author, the publisher, show the scriptural reference where appropriate and not edit the item. You may delete or substitute the title to better suit your use. (Titles here and in collections of homilies are used [by me] to facilitate referencing and tracking materials. I do not use them in workshops or in preaching.) Where you see (BCP) cited the reference is to the Anglican *Book of Common Prayer* (usually, Episcopal Church, USA.)

Most of these pieces are scripturally based or inspired. If you are not familiar with the scripture referenced, I suggest you check it out before reading the item. Some of the quirkiness or humor of scripture will then, I believe, be more evident, relevant and appreciated.

Many years ago, I attended a workshop led by the great Saul Alinski, noted for his pioneering work in community organization. His field was bold, controversial and personally very risky. His background was criminology (University of Chicago) and philosophy of American Democracy. His aim in life was to empower neighborhoods to improve their lot through participation in the political arena. Yes, a very controversial and dangerous way of life

At one point in the workshop, someone asked him: "Mr. Alinski, if you were to see your vision of democracy actually working, *then* what would you want to do?" His reply was unhesitant: "Spend my time on music, art and poetry, which is what we were meant to be doing all along." Clearly this was something to which he had given some serious thought. His adamant reply resonated within me, especially the "this is what we're meant to be doing!" part.

If we waited until things were all settled before practicing any art, we'd have no masterpieces in music or painting or architecture or sculpturing or poetry. The practice of any of the arts seems, when viewed against the dire needs of so many of our global neighbors, to be purely luxurious, extravagant, or downright selfish. I'm sure one could say something like that about my call, which is to ordained Christian ministry. Yet, I've spent my life responding to that call.

In the context of that vocation, poetry it has seemed to me is a luxury I've seldom felt free to invest myself in. I've had many interests in my lifetime and have pursued many. Poetry has always been in the mix. But it had to wait for the frailty of increasing years to slow my pace and open the time needed for thought and composure. So, with profound respect and consideration for Mr. Alinski's point, I dare invite you to indulge anyway, and may God bless this extravagant investment of yourself.

Charles R. Wilson

Prologue: John 1:1-18

LOGOS

The Word was the Beginning;
there was no-time before.
        But God was.
Even in no-time God was.
Word and God were One in no-time.

Then God thought (in no-time for thinking),
"Something ought to Be."
            But with no-time for Enduring
            And no-place to Be
how could anything Become?
So God invented Existence.

In Existence, Something could be for a while and in a place
without being forever and everywhere.
But this required space-time (which was not-yet).
        So God Spoke the Word.
        Clocks ran, Reality Began.
Suns, planets, days, forests, streams, meadows, armadillos and us,
        all by the Word of God.

But then a new "reality," separation!
Things enduring for a while and in a place
        have Existence, not Being
        and attendant flaws and limits.
So God speaks Word anew. And that Word is New-Being.
So it is that Being itself takes Reality into itself
        and the Word becomes Flesh.
        Separation: conquered!

1

O God, the author of peace and lover of concord, to know you is eternal life and to serve you is perfect freedom: Defend us, your humble servants, in all assaults of our enemies; that we, surely trusting in your defense, may not fear the power of any adversaries; through the might of Jesus Christ our Lord. Amen
  (BCP)

Heavenly Father, in you we live and move and have our being: We humbly pray you so to guide and govern us by your Holy Spirit, that in all the cares and occupations of our life we may not forget you, but remember that we are ever walking in your sight; through Jesus Christ our Lord. Amen
  (BCP)

THE PARTNER IDEA

At first there was nothing – all dark to the core;
      no boundaries, no beaches, here, there or before.
A vacuum unbounded by mountain or shore,
      an abyss in the midst of a void, nothing more.

An idea grew out of that nothing at all,
      that something should be on this tiny black ball.
So God made the stones and the mountains so tall,
      the streams and the wind and the lightening, et al.

God made all the islands and broad, restless seas,
      the beaches and sand bars and deep ocean trenches.
He made it mysterious with moonlight and breeze,
      an enigmatical climate untamed and relentless.

God backed off and looked over all he had made;
      felt justified pride in the crafting he'd done.
Like an artist who titles his painting when through,
      God labeled his art work *The Beautiful Blue.*

Restless, like most of us deep in creating,
      God hankered for color in his art awaking.
So God made the flowers and bushes and trees,
      the grasses and cacti and broad fertile leas.

Now green shared with blue as the prominent stripe,
      but the truly new, duly created was *life.*
Once just an idea, now here and a beaut.
      God paused once again to review and compute.

It still needs fine tuning, God mused as he pondered.
        Motion and action would add cool attraction.
God acted again and came up with the whales,
        with ponies and monkeys and apes with no tails.

He made all the birds that fly through the air,
        the reptiles and fishes and stuff like that there.
He made cats and kittens, a dog and her pup,
        and buzzards to keep all creation cleaned up.

Then God recollected all he had done,
        daring and risky but also great fun.
Now mobile and beautiful, colorful and living
        a joyful adventure in creative giving.

Now one more ingredient before we let go:
        God saw no one there who could possibly know
his joy and his pleasure in crafting this show
        and no one to care about where it would go.

"So far no one's shared in the pleasures I've seen
        in forming the whole of this colorful scheme.
In short, no one cares that I've been a'creating.
        There's nothing here capable of such ruminating.

"We must have a creature in here self-aware,
        one that will know me and one that will care."
He thought that one over, came up with a pair.
        God called us his *partners* right then and right there.

He offered a covenant defining our role
        so we would remember what we are here for.
To glorify him as we play at our soundings,
        he blessed us with senses to know our surroundings.

Now we sally forth in wisdom and freedom,
    the highest achievement of all he created;
not lackeys, not slaves or not mute critters we,
    but partners in crafting what's now going to be.

CONFESSION

Why is it confession's connected with *shame*?
    And *guilt* is assumed if there's someone to blame?
Confession can also proclaim truth and good,
    and guilt as a good as one does what one should.

Confession is also the subject of creeds.
    To live by our creed is good living indeed.
And then to be blamed for our faith, hope and love
    is guilt in the virtues as judged from above.

So terms like confession and guilt and the like
    should get a fair shake in our regular banter.
Creation's not made out of negative chatter;
    the plusses excel in all cases that matter.

5

HYDRAULICS, INC.
THE WATER WORKS

Water no doubt was already about
  when our Father jump-started Creation.
No one to report to, he appointed himself
  the Hydraulics Coordinator.

He set out immediately to structure the stuff
  with islands and beaches, a dome up above.
He would use his position to gloat on our winnings,
  or to express his contempt for our sinnings.

A partner and friend was what the Lord wanted
  as he brooded there over the water.
The Company of Heaven was far too amenable,
  an incredible lack of ideas commendable.

Archangels and angels there followed God's say
  with nary a doubt or a question . . . or
even creative suggestion! With followers like that,
  leading can be far too boring to mention!

Yes, a partner and friend with a will of its own
  in command of its own ability!
Water would be the primary ingredient
  with dust sprinkled in for stability.

With God's breath of life he would fill it with spirit!
  Over eons of time he got it all going
with myriads of creatures like you.
  It was good by and large, though quite risky too!

In the Sweet Gum Tree

With corruption erupting right there in the brew,
        it soon became clear that a new start was due.
It was time once again to free chaos up,
        then let it have at a creation corrupt.

God unleashed the waters above and below
        and he flooded every damned nation.
However, he waffled a bit on his bet
        and preserved an ark-load of creation.

Noah and family survived that deluge
        along with their boatload of fauna.
They spread to and fro and re-peopled that land
        from the Nile to the hills of Nevada.

They sated their thirst at a spring or a well
        or from streams of clear running waters.
They washed off their bodies and mended their wounds,
        and nurtured their sons and their daughters.

Eventually stuck, stomping clay, straw and muck
        near the Pharaoh's hot brick baking ovens,
they were saved by a babe hid out in the water,
        rescued by Pharaoh's fair, bare-legged daughter.

Destined to be the prime prince of his people
        and saving them from their tormentors,
Moses plagued the Egyptians, demanded his freedom
        and ran off with their treasured mementos.

He marched from the Nile, then crossed the Red Sea
        without getting anyone wet,
brought the whole band to the Promised Land
        not even impacting the national debt.

In time, John the Baptist appeared on the scene
 calling all souls to repent and believe.
He dunked those who came in the cold, muddy stream;
 sin carried away, the people now clean.

When our Savior dropped by John dunked him in there too!
 In the name of the Trinity, we're blessed as well,
given our names and marked with a seal.
 But, dunk, pour or dip, water clinches the deal.

Now scientists are out there scanning the heavens,
 searching the galaxies, planets and spheres;
seeking a world our people might live on,
 recruiting explorers and brave pioneers.

As in ages gone by, give us bold folk and brave
 to scout out new lands and domains.
To discover new wealth that our people may thrive,
 including new challenges for which we might strive.

Not silver or gold, not diamonds or pearls,
 nor bounty of pirates or spoil of explorers.
Not a land flowing with sweet milk and honey,
 nor rich in crude oil, or plenty of money.

But give us a land with green grass and broad valleys,
 hard-wooded forests and meadows of clover.
Bless us with livestock and plenty of fodder
 with rivers and streams of fresh flowing water.

What do you think? An enormous adventure
 calling for courage like never before?
Shall this be our purpose? Is this what we're meant for?
 Check out our Hydraulics Coordinator!

THE KING'S ARRIVAL

The earth is the Lord's and all that is in it,
    the world and all people who dwell thereupon.
It was he who had raised it up out of the sea,
    on the rivers, created and called it to be.

Who dares to climb up on his holy mountain;
    who ventures to stand on this sod?
It is those who are pure of heart and of hand,
    not obliged to a lie or pledged to a fraud.

These are the ones to be blessed by the Lord
    blessed by our God of salvation.
It is this generation who seek out the Lord;
    they are the ones to be blessed and adored.

Lift up your heads, swing wide your gates,
    hold them on high and don't bolt the doors.
Swing wide the posterns and clear up the floors.
    King-Glory is ready to enter our quarters.

And who is this eminent King-Glory, pray tell?
    It's the Lord armed and ready for battle.
Awake, all of you asleep at your posts.
    Stay alert you dreamy and numb, dozing city.

King-Glory's at hand with his grand angel band,
    his armies all ready to take firm command.
Be ready to greet him with gates open wide.
    King-Glory is here and has now come inside.

OUR MISSION
The End of the Beginning of the Gospel
of Christ Jesus the one Son of God

There was a chill in the air, and gripped in despair
    we arrived in our drab mourning habits.
It was dawn on that very first day of the week.
    All the guys had run off like scared rabbits.

It was now up to us to attend to affairs,
    there was only one lingering question:
We were willing and all, but all on our own?
    How can we remove that huge rolling stone?

But we looked and the tomb had already been breached.
    We entered and found, not the one who had died
but an angel in white who addressed us like this,
    "You're looking for Jesus the crucified.

"See? Here is where they laid him;
    the place is now vacant. But wait, I'm not through.
The Master's here with us, his mission continues.
    You'll meet at the lake, as he already told you."

We nearly collapsed, faint and in terror;
    baffled, bewildered in wonder and dread.
But seeing our errand was basically finished
    and ignoring his orders, we fled!

And that's the end of Mark's beginning,
    of the Good News of Jesus the Christ.
The continuing saga demands faith and trust,
    But according to Mark, that is now up to us!

In the Sweet Gum Tree

Merciful God:
We confess that we have sinned against you
    in thought, word and deed
    by what we have, and have not done.
We have not totally loved you.
We have not loved our neighbors or ourselves.
We are truly sorry and humbly repent.
        For the sake of your son
        have mercy and forgive
                that we may delight in your will
                and walk in your way
                to the glory of your name.
                        Amen

A Red-shouldered Hawk

Genesis 18:22-33

CHALLENGING GOD

In heavenly spheres the matter was settled:
 The Lord would go down, and wipe out those two towns.
Evil was rampant; the people were shameless.
 The only way out: total annihilation!

But here on the earth we were still undecided.
 Abraham, diplomatically, stepped up before God.
"Are you going to count *all* of those folk wicked fools
 just because their two cities are slimy cesspools?

"Suppose there are fifty you still could call righteous
 in the grimy slum quarters of that evil city,
to castigate all of the villains among them,
 will you also wipe out every one of those fifty?

"Far be it for you, as you claim to be just,
 to slay all the blameless while judging the cad!
Far be that for you to treat all souls alike
 so the just are condemned right along with the bad.

"So, what is your word? Should the judge of the cosmos
 not do what is just, right here on the earth?
Should not fifty righteous be salvaged this day?
 Are you going to just trash your good name away?"

The Lord God responded to Abe then and there,
 "If I find fifty decent in that wicked city
I will surely renege on my intended action
 and spare the whole town for the sake of the fifty."

In the Sweet Gum Tree

The Patriarch replied, "I'm but ashes and dust,
        but pray you allow me to speak one more time.
"Hey, suppose that, say five of the fifty are wanting.
        Will you ravage that town for the lack of just five?"

God countered, "I will not destroy if I find forty-five there."
        But yet again Abe just as boldly replied,
"So, maybe you find only forty souls then?"
        "For the sake of the forty I will not destroy them."

"Let the Lord not be angry, ah right? If I speak just this
        one more time. Suppose that you find only thirty are there?"
He responded, "Morality there is exceedingly rare.
        I will certainly refrain if a mere thirty are there."

"May I presume to press the point further already?
        Suppose there are twenty there found?"
"For the sake of just twenty I'll still show them pity.
        Show me twenty good folk and I'll spare the whole city."

"Oh let the Lord not be irate with me, fine?
        If I dare to speak out now on ill-borrowed time?
Your servant is nothing but dirt on your feet
        and audacious to dare even now then to speak.

"But suppose then you find only ten righteous men?"
        The Lord patiently countered yet once again,
"For the sake of the ten I will not destroy it!
        Show me just ten; I'll spare *all* of them then."

Thus the Lord ended his speaking with Abraham
        and continued down his holy way.
Abe finished up too, and then covering his face
        our patriarch turned and went back to his place.

BALAAM'S BALKY DONKEY

We knew they were coming to raid us.
    All beasts in the field now had heard.
A "tsunami" o'er whelming the coast line!
    We should stop them? Don't be absurd!

They had God's mighty favor on their side;
    neither brass gods nor hex could deter.
So curse away Balak, God's blessing precedes you,
    your jinx is naught but a bore.

We were sent to a different location,
    a narrower view so they thought.
When an angel with sword blocked the pathway,
    an alternate route then was sought.

Though he beat on my back, I continued to balk.
    (What's a seeing-eye beast s'posed to do?)
Till I lay down beneath him none else saw the sword there,
    all ready to whack us in two!

Then clearing my throat I beseeched him,
    "Is this the way I should be won?
Your enduring and faithful old mount since your youth,
    you owe some respect for the run!

"Want to get us both killed up ahead?
    Then open your eyes to the view.
I am doing my job for your and my safety.
    Yes I'm balking, but not just for you."

In the Sweet Gum Tree

So my friends now I look for your wisdom.
        Consider my current impasse.
Given all of this mortal stupidity
        including their gods made of brass.

Considering these dummies who cannot see angels
        and allowing room for their sass,
why should I take this all uncomplaining?
        Why should it be *me* that they call, "Balaam's ass?"

VENITE

Come, let us sing to the Lord! Let us bellow for joy
    to the Rock of our salvation.
Let us come before him with psalms of thanksgiving;
      let them ring out aloud through the entire nation.

His hand holds the canyons and mountains he formed;
    He is King above all of the gods!
The sea is his playground, the hills and the prairies
    all glorify God their Creator.

We bow now our heads and bend our knees
    before Yahweh, our Maker and Friend.
We are the sheep of his fertile pasture;
    it's to his voice alone that we now attend!

In the Sweet Gum Tree

Dedicated to Lloyd Gressle, 1975

OUR BISHOP

Who do we love and ever stand by?
Who is our champion, for whom would we die?
(Well, you can skip that) He's a pretty cool guy.
Our Bishop

Who has our loyalty forever and ever?
A challenger always; a critic—never!
When faced with the big tasks, who is our lever?
Our Bishop

Who holds us up when we can't cope?
Gives confidence, love, strength, hope?
And sends us on looking like a dope?
Our Bishop

A born leader, competent, effective (they said)
took over the reins from a man named Fred
then slammed the diocese into the red!
Our Bishop

From problems in Easton to those that are Sayre's,
headaches and heartaches, layers and layers.
Who has the answer? (A glass and three Bayers)
Our Bishop

While committee and task force, Council and group
charge on faithfully through fire-ringed hoop,
who's sitting at home enjoying Marg's soup?
Our Bishop

A great preacher—a teacher—a spirit lifter,
but who would be lost—a zero—a drifter,
without Doersam and Faga, Sweet, Paul and Shifter?
Our Bishop

He loves the rich and the poor, the old and the mod,
rubs elbows with princes, men of the sod.
Why, we once even caught him, talking with God.
Our Bishop

But when truth and justice have few buyers
who is it who's feared by scoundrels and liars,
as he cruises the diocese putting out fires?
Our Bishop

And when at last his days are through
and he's gone to meet the friends he knew,
who will quench the fires in that place too?
Our Bishop

O God, the King eternal, whose light divides the day from the night and turns the shadows of death into the morning: Drive from us all wrong desires, incline our hearts to keep your law, and guide our feet into the way of peace; that, having done your will with cheerfulness during the day, we may, when night comes, rejoice to give you thanks; through Jesus Christ our Lord. Amen.
(BCP)

Luke 15:11-32

TWO BROTHERS

There was a widower rancher on a spread over by Lander,
  raising two boys on his own.
His sons were his pride and his hope for the future;
  the sun rose and set on those two lads alone.
Both had their duties in minding the cattle
  and both their assignments at home.

  While one youth was lacking in personal drive
  had scarcely a hint of imagination,
  the other had courage and plenty of vision
  but no sense whatever of true dedication.

One morning while feasting on eggs, steak and flapjacks,
  the younger one tossed them a bomb.
"Pop," he announced, "I'm fed up with ranching.
  I want to get out on my own.
I've long since outgrown my cowboy romances.
  Wyoming's no longer my home.

  "I need fulfillment, a taste of the action!
  I'm fed up-to-here in this lonely lair.
  So give, if you please my share of inheritance
  and I'll be the first to get out of your hair!"

All present were shocked – this astounding demand –
  but, he only asked for his share.
They finally assented, so Pop hocked the ranch
  to finance the foolish kid's flair.
The lad packed his stuff in his Lincoln convertible
  and soon whisked himself right out of there.

19

He landed in Vegas and quickly drew to him
a host of wild friends with lots of advice.
Soon out of cash-money then bereft of all friends,
blew the last of his cash on a toss of the dice.

Experienced in ranching, he took to the country
for some way to eke out a living.
A swine-farm combine on the outskirts of town
had a deal with most Los Vegas kitchens.
They salvaged the scrapings from those fancy dishes
and hauled them away without any hitches.

With a minimum of treating the stuff was made ready
for diners with no taste at all.
For slopping the hogs (minimum wage, no benefits)
Was the lad's new "executive position."

It didn't take long, reviewing conditions
to see how much better his father's help fared.
When he came to himself, he vowed to go back there
and beg for a job as a simple ranch hand.
A cowboy in Wyoming, it was now that much clearer,
had a heap better deal in his life off the land

than a starving sty-keeper deep down in the south
with nary a hope of forgiveness.
The compassionate father saw him off at a distance,
and ran out to greet him with hugs and with kisses.

He gave him a silver belt buckle, a Pendleton shirt and a Stetson,
a pair of brand new Lachaise boots,
then butchered a prime beef, retained some musicians
and invited his friends for a party and toot.
The elder brother was out punching cattle
when all of this fuss of reunion commenced.

Approaching the house and hearing the ruckus
he called to a cowhand to ask of meaning.
Deeply offended at the errant kid's treatment,
he adamantly refused to join in the preening.

The father came out and tried to persuade him,
    "Your brother was lost and has now come around.
It's like he who was dead has now come to life,
    let's go and make merry! Your brother is found!"
The elder boy, stubborn, livid and mad,
    backed off and stood tall and proud.

    "Given *my* history and your son's wild living
    midst harlots and thieves, in brothels and bars,
    it's high time, at minimum, for *me* to be given
    a kid and a keg for a bash with *my* pals."

The father was grieved at this animosity and tried to argue his case.
    "Son, all that is mine is yours as you know,
but we must celebrate and rejoice. This brother of yours
    was dead and now lives; he was lost and now he is found.
This is not about balancing trivial accounts
    but of love and of family reunion."

    Now this is a tale of two siblings.
    The steady one, short on drive and ambition,
    the prodigal, lacking in true dedication.
    So, I ask you then, which of these brothers
        exemplifies your situation?

FOUNDATIONS

A wise man went forth to build a new home.
 He found the right site with a view all around
on an outcrop of rock near a spring in the ground.
 He laid out his form for the mortar and stone
 for a building fair, square, plumb and level.

A fool went out back to throw up a shack.
 He chanced on a sandbar downstream from the track
near plenty of water not terribly deep.
 He framed up his hovel with mud, straw and shovel,
 a shelter in inclement weather.

A storm front blew in from out of the north.
 The lightning struck trees and tore up their branches.
Ill winds raged all over the meadows and ranches.
 They beat upon two recent structures en route,
 slamming them hither and round and about.

When the tempest had passed on out of the region,
 one house remained on that now tranquil scene.
The shack had collapsed and washed down the ravine!
 On making your name there is this gentle rule:
 build wisely on rock and not like that fool.

QUEEN ESTHER'S BANQUET

Spirits were high, the guests were all merry
    when Queen Vashti offended the king.
He had ordered his eunuchs to parade her proud beauty
    for a stupidly drunk and fumbling ring.

She steadfastly refused to be so vilely used
    as a teasing, tempting, sex-object as branded.
She slammed her foot down, latched her front door,
    and the eunuchs came home empty-handed.

An enraged, plastered king called out for review
    by his Imperial Corps of Tabloid Reporters.
None could remember an affront such as this,
    a queen contravening her monarch's clear orders.

This outrageous offense could become a new pattern,
    if blathered about from maiden to maiden.
The practice itself must be nipped in the bud
    and due order preserved in the kingdom.

The Reviewers determined that Vashti must go
    (a new Law of the Persians and Medes).
The clear implication throughout the whole nation:
    "All gals must comply with their guy's stupid pleas."

Thus began a wide search for a worthy new queen,
    the criterion: *exceptional splendor*.
Fair virgins were placed in the harem for checking
    with months to prime, primp and prepare for.

23

All brand name cosmetics, lipsticks and rouges
　　　brought booths for displaying their ware.
Each contestant had multiple eunuchs and ladies
　　　attending her charms and then grooming her hair.

Esther was one of the fair lovelies discovered;
　　　she totally eclipsed all the rest.
Her complexion was dazzling, her figure to-die-for.
　　　Of all beauties there, not even a contest!

However there was one perplexing condition:
　　　Esther was foreign, and Jewish, at that.
The king didn't care about ethnic verity.
　　　But advisors latched on to that Jew fact.

Esther meantime was beloved and adored;
　　　her increasing fame and acclaim wouldn't quit.
A party was planned, dignitaries invited;
　　　it would be called the *Queen Esther Banquet.*

Now Mordecai was Queen Esther's first cousin
　　　and also her surrogate father.
He stood by near the gate as a beggar and spy,
　　　a fine spot to tune in on all palace blather.

It was here he discovered two disgruntled eunuchs
　　　arranging a royal elimination.
With Esther right there as a readymade contact
　　　he quietly shared all this mole information.

She discreetly leaked the dastardly scheme
　　　starting a Federal Bureau Inspection.
Essentials confirmed, they were tried and condemned
　　　and two traitors swung from the King's handy scaffold.

Haman, by appointment Secretary of State
    reputed to be the King's Man.
He was proud of his invite to Queen Esther's Banquet
    and strutted his stuff as, "The Queen's Special Fan."

Haman was also an open Jew Hater,
    Supreme Honkey Dorkie in his local Klan.
Quite unaware of the queen's ethnicity
    he charged on ahead with his lethal plan.

He had already constructed a seventy foot gallows
    so zealous was he and so sure of his plan,
expecting to hang that Mordecai on it
    once he had finished with slandering the man.

The Jew still hung out there, a throbbing sore thumb,
    not attending to Haman's proud presence,
enraging the fool beyond human endurance,
    disgracefully offensive to his hazy senses.

Haman's intention, pure evil unaltered,
    to lock up that Jew in the slammer.
then go and annihilate all Jews in the land.
    Mordecai would be gone in the clamor.

Through evil deceit and conniving
    the order was royally passed.
An official date was accordingly set
    for the plan's expeditious enactment.

The delicate protocol for approaching the king
    involved risk of death for any who dared.
Esther, at first, was inclining toward caution
    but Mordecai hard-pressed her to up and take action.

"Sweet Esther, God works in mysterious ways.
    Could be you've come into your royal position
for just such a time as this!"
    Esther thus challenged would not be remiss.

"Now get the word out to all of our people,
    to join my attendants and me
in personal prayer and a discipline of fasting.
    And pray that our faith prove to be everlasting."

All Jews in the realm mourned in sackcloth and ashes,
    in fasting and then common prayer,
"That our cause be well served and our people preserved
    through God's intervening pro-action."

As it happened, the king in reviewing his files
    recalled an encounter with would-be assassins.
He also remembered no award had been made
    to the one who had issued that caution.

Wishing to fix this unfortunate lapse,
    he summoned his top Cabinet Officer.
"Mr. Secretary," he innocently queried proud Haman,
    "What should be done to reward a good man,

one whom the Sovereign desires to honor?"
    He pondered the query from the king's perspective.
Who could that dude be but Haman himself?
    The conniving Haman spoke up and responded:

"Nothing's too good for such a one
    as the one the king wishes to honor.
Don him in ermine and robe him in red;
    let a gold crown embellish his head.

"Grant him a eunuch who'll bow down and scrape
    and come running at his every beckon and call.
Give him a pure-bred Arabian stallion from
    the finest in your royal stall.

"That's what the king really should do
    for the one the king wishes to honor."
The monarch appeared inordinately pleased
    with the council that he had received.

"You go see to it!" he directed proud Haman.
    "Mordecai is the prince that I have in mind!"
That mortified Haman; he stuttered, he stammered,
    his choppers fell out of his mouth.

He was fit to be tied, he just about died
    but he was stuck and obliged to see the deed done.
Haman dutifully escorted the Jew, Mordecai
    royally decked out as the King's number one.

Up and down the town square parading
    Haman embarrassingly proclaiming:
"See what is done for that special one,
    the one the king wishes to honor!"

The big day arrived. It was Queen Esther's Banquet;
    they gathered from throughout the realm.
The bash would continue for nearly a week with
    Queen Esther's beauty displayed at the helm.

The king himself was feeling no pain;
    his spirit was leaping like fire.
He called out "Queen Esther," so all there could hear it,
    "I intend to grant you, your foremost desire.

"You name it, you've got it, to the half of my kingdom.
     We celebrate you on this festive week.
So, Queen Esther what is your fondest wish?"
     The Queen eyed the crowd, "Here's what I seek,"

(Then she paused just a tad to cash in on the moment.)
     "A law has been passed which has the effect
of slaughtering all of my people. No trials, no judges!
     Plain extermination, a cultural mass annihilation!"

The King was dumbfounded, "Who'd do such a thing?
     We'll rectify that directive immediately!
Who is the rat who issued that order?"
     (They noticed that Haman was leaking all over.)

She pointed her finger, "There is your man
     wearing your crest. He's the Jew-hater!"
Haman clumsily staggered all over the flat,
     stumbling across the queen's private futon,

begging her mercy, and in that awkward act,
     provoking the king even further.
Clutching and groping he struggled for balance,
     knocked over the candles and crashed to the floor.

The king shouted out, "See! Look at him grapple
     right here with my queen in my personal parlor.
Hang him!" A eunuch stepped up volunteering,
     "There's a gallows already in Haman's back yard."

They strung Haman up on the scaffold he built
     to hang Mordecai the Jew on.
The people were saved; Holocaust was averted!
     Esther's a hero and Haman is gone.

John 5:1-14

FAITH HEALING

He had wrestled the Mineral Springs pool line for years;
        "Please give me a break," he prayed through his tears.
But whenever the waters beaconed and stirred,
        the bullies brushed by him and offensively cursed,
        "Look out old man we're going in first!"

The Lord passing by took note of the cast;
        Suggested he skip all that hassle.
It wasn't effective, at least not for him.
        Alternative medicine might work a lot faster,
        "Take up your mat and go home."

A lawyer came down, sized up the scenario,
        outraged and just seething with wrath.
"Hey," called the Law. "Your move is illegal.
        We have a rule on traveling this path.
        No toting your bed on the Sabbath!"

The Lord couldn't fathom their silly legalities.
        "My Father is still laboring on," countered he.
"My calling compels me to bless and to heal.
        And here is where healing is needed.
        I must pause to heed a brother in need."

Some kids hanging out on a corner nearby
        took note of these curious proceedings. Then
one lad called out to the intruding lawyer,
        "Hey, Mister Law, with a doctor's degree,
        can the obstructing, the patient's home free!"

JOB'S EASTER

Have pity O my friends, have pity,
  for the hand of God has touched me!
I should shout out with joy from the mountain top.
  I could fashion my words into solid rock
  with a hammer and tempered cold-chisel

O that they were engraved over there
  on a towering Vermont granite mountain.
Or carved right here in a solid oak panel
  to assure they are with us forever.

For now I know my redeemer's alive;
  at the last he will stand on this sod.
And when this body has turned into dust
  here at my side and with my own eyes
  I shall, O so boldly, behold my true God.

From ghoulies and ghosties, long leggitie beasties and things that go bump in the night; Good Lord deliver us.
    (BCP; The Litany – a very early edition)

Mark 12:29-31

ULTIMATE REALITY

It has been said that LOVE and HATE
  are precisely exactly the opposite,
as in north and south or east and west
  on someone's emotional-compass.

It could even be (metaphorically speaking),
  heaven and hell in their final wrest!
Or some other sort of moody extreme
  in somebody's parallel universe.

In this kind of reckoning, these two extremes
  are seen as opposite poles,
not average or mean or something between,
  of people's wide range of their feelings.

But that doesn't cut it; it misses the point.
  Mere "feeling" just doesn't rate.
Love is defined as what's *Ultimately Real.*
  The opposite of that would be *Finally Fake.*

But hate is no fake, its reality too!
  It's considered a dangerous infection
distressing a heart meant for truth, peace and joy,
  corrupting our thinking-being-intention.

Hate's a displaced, voracious negation,
  drowning with vengeance our faint mortal voices.
It may be a void with regard to Reality
  but hate's a reality in our mortal choices.

If these two are feelings, is there really a choice?
        One doesn't reach feeling through conscious decision.
And if feelings aren't functions of pondering and choosing
        they are out of control, beyond our perusing!

So, do love and hate claim equal validity?
        And if that is the case, do *we* rate them the same?
I can't believe where this logic leads us.
        With this kind of thinking there's no one to blame!

Love is the life-force God planted within us,
        a gift of the Spirit for eternal connection.
A positive power in tune with our calling,
        seeking reunion of that which has parted.

Love is the essence of Godly reality,
        uniting all that for which all hearts were crafted.
Love is eternal and certainly no stranger;
        it's precisely the how and the why we're crafted.

Love levels the highway and evens the bumps,
        a smooth autobahn through the jungle.
It clears out the boulders and fills in the ruts,
        so travel's not merely a rumble.

Hate gets us bogged down in the clay and the muck,
        wreaks havoc with all our emotions.
It clutters the pathway with all kinds of junk,
        causing our runners to stumble.

Love makes us open, clean and accessible,
        responsive, uncluttered, present and glad.
Hate makes us brittle, hard and insensible,
        repulsive, ridged, abusive and sad.

Love is with being as hate is with dying.
  Love is what is, as hate is negation.
Love is to living as hate is to death.
  Love is to hugging as hate is rejection.

We don't control love and we don't possess it.
  It well may persuade us and we might be in it,
but love's not a tool we can hire or master.
  And love's not a substance we paint with or plaster.

But once we are in it, *we* are the tool.
  Love drives the program. Love is the master.
Then our option is take it or leave it
  where "leave it" equates with "disaster."

So, emotions or feelings or principles for dealings;
  both love and hate are forever here with us.
That's not to say they should rate equal weight.
  They are as different as early and late.

For with day, light is with us; with night it is missing.
  One is a presence, the other an absence.
Love as in being, ultimately is where hate in finality is truly fake.
  So now don't you see it? We finally got it!

Love in its being is where IS really is.
  While hate doesn't rate, being that hate truly ain't.
So if one's to be, never mind all the qualities,
  Being-in-Love is the only True State!

Jesus said, "The first commandment is this: Hear, O Israel: The Lord our God is
  the only Lord. Love the Lord your God with all your heart, with all your soul,
  with all your mind, and with all your strength. The second is this: Love your
  neighbor as yourself. There is no other commandment greater than these."

THE CENTURIAN'S FAITH

He said: "O My Lord, I had no intention
of interrupting your day.
I had only hoped for the power of your Word
to cure my sick slave on the way.

"For I understand about rank and authority
and have troops under my command.
I order one to come and another to go
and they come and they go as I demand.

"I am not worthy to host you, my Lord
and do not presume to delay you.
Only speak the word, the healing is done,
and my servant will join me tomorrow."

The Lord was amazed at this witness of faith.
This foreigner had got it. He had seen the light.
"If only my followers would get it like this
our cause would catch fire, our mission take flight."

In the Sweet Gum Tree

Inspired by Charlene's wedding involving rings made of an exotic alloy

HANDS AND BANDS

Kneading the dough and baking the bread,
    Often abused, usually red.
Stirring in yeast, folding in flour,
    productive today, arthritic tomorrow.

Working full time, from morning to night
    scrubbing the floor, making things bright,
vacuuming carpets, hauling out dirt,
    smoothing the linens, folding a shirt.

    Left hand, third finger, is proper 'tis said
    for bands of pewter, tin, gold or lead.
    Showing you're bound one to another,
    husband and wife; tear not asunder!

Cleaning the bathroom, scouring the sink,
    changing the diaper, fetching a drink.
Kissing it better, soothing the bruise,
    singing a lullaby, tying her shoes.

Mowing and hoeing, repairing the car,
    fixing storm windows, opening the jar,
pulling up weeds and cleaning the cellar,
    hands getting calloused, scarred, even yeller!

    His hands are larger than hers, so we've seen.
    Can't really be sure, they're so seldom clean.
    She wears a seven, he takes eleven
    wipe off the grease to see the band better.

35

Richer or poorer, sickness and health,
    swearing their vows, pledging their wealth.
Sealing the covenant before all the witnesses,
    passing the peace and sharing the kissesses.

Intimate tendencies should set the course,
    loving intentions, no need for force!
Uncommon devotion, each to the other,
    rings claim fidelity with one's true lover.

    Strike up the band, bring on the fiddle
    lend me your ear, hear now my riddle:
    If bands and kisses pledge high-flyin' attitude,
    what's with the garter? A promise of latitude?

Isaiah 2:3-5

LIGHT OF THE LORD

The Word of the Lord charges forth out of Zion,
  a notice of judgment on nations today.
Our God arbitrates among all of his people;
  he teaches us now how to walk in his way.

And so we proceed under guidance of God
  to beat all our swords into plowshares.
To forge all our spears into pruning hooks,
  and not raise a hand against anyone's land.

We shall not partake of war-making here-on.
  We walk in the paths of our Lord.
Factory and ingot, machine shop and grease,
  now fully employed in the interest of peace.

ON ALERT

Out of the deep I cry to you Lord.
     I pray that you heed my petition.
If you were to judge us on all our transgressions,
     Lord, whoever could stand up to that?

But that is not how we have known you.
     Mercy is more to your natural leaning
and forgiveness your normal proceeding.
     We wait for you Lord; we're holding our breath.

More alert than the guards on their morning watch,
     is how we wait for you, Oh our Lord and our God.
We wait for your love and redemption,
     confident your grace will renew us.

Numbers 11:26-30

OUTSIDE THE TENT

Moses was in an unusual position,
    he one-on-one literally reported to God.
The campers, an angry and quarrelsome lot,
    just odd drifting transients, not men of the sod.

Moses chose seventy, lined 'em up single file
    inside the tent and on down the wall.
The Glory of God swept through that assembly
    and the charisma of Moses descended on all.

The gift so it seems, not an enduring strain,
    lasted but twenty four hours.
So the seventy preached for merely a day,
    the maximum span of their powers.

But some of that juice leaked outside the tent
    infecting two bystanding others
who were ripe for the call, caught a full dose
    and proceeded to teach all their brothers.

Eldad and Medad were book-thumping prophets
    and oh my how they could preach!
They could stir up a crowd and keep them spellbound,
    infrequently suffering a breach.

They were inspired, charismatic, with depth and conviction;
    they seized nearly every new session.
With awe and respect, spoke powerfully direct,
    dynamic, dramatic, no question!

39

However they did have detractors.
    Some wanted to see their credentials.
"Show us your license! Let's see your diploma!
    How do we know you're professionals?

"You're from outside the tent. You are not one of us.
    You're not cleared to preach in the camp!
Your tippet's not black, book's too thin to thump
    and you haven't much oil in your lamp.

"How can you expect from us due respect
    when you feast on locusts and honey,
then charge on ahead preaching justice and hope
    in a world that's not all that sunny?

"When we know the truth, the truth that enslaves us,
    existence is truly not rosy!
The world's hell-on-earth, a speck in the cosmos,
    and you two are a little too cozy!"

So they formally charged the evangelists
    and filed a complaint with Chief Moses.
They threatened a strike and a sympathy walk-out
    while Eldad and Medad kept teaching.

"Do unto others," they quietly admonished,
    "as you would have them do to you."
A few of them heard. A few were astonished,
    such preaching right out of the blue?

In the Sweet Gum Tree

The program continued there outside the tent,
     with dancing and spirit-filled tunes.
Detractors persisted, "Collar's too high. Chasuble's gaudy,
     and your thongs were created for sand dunes.

"Your voice is too quiet, your tie is too loud,
     and you're not near as tall as our previous teacher.
You're too legalistic, non-pharisaic,
     not nearly as meek as our beloved late preacher."

Yet tenure in this camp is limited.
     And "a prophet's not heard in a town he calls home."
There are other communes and other tent camps,
     and preachers must preach in them also.

Our evangelists set off for a city called Nazareth
     hoping to come a bit wiser.
Eventually to claim enduring fame
     as associates of John the Baptizer.

But Eldad and Medad, ordained on the spot
     as Moses affirmed them with pride.
"Would that all of our people be prophets like these
     taking the word far and wide."

Since then it has not been required by God
     to carry a staff or see waters parted.
If we thump and we dunk and we walk as they talk,
     well, that's how we Baptists got started.

It's the people telling their stories that gives the Gospel its wings to fly.
                              Bishop Kivengeri

41

SAFE HAVEN

The Lord is our haven. Our God is our strength;
    a presence when we face storm, conflict or threat.
Though earthquake and flood's raging waters beseech us,
    though mountains and hills shake, crumble, collapse
we will not fear danger nor flee for behold:

    The Lord is here with us,
    his angels our fort.

The river refreshes and cleanses God's city.
    It's God's domicile and his presence rules here.
From dawn and then on we bask in his pity.
    Kings threaten and bluster, are armed and defiant.
Our earth is subdued, at peace and compliant.

    The Lord is here with us,
    his angels our fort.

See for yourself, his awesome peace-making.
    He disarms the bullies; he buries their tanks.
He crushes the fortified cities he's taken.
    So calm you down now, find peace and be saved.
Our God is our refuge and he will be praised.

    The Lord is here with us,
    his angels our fort.

Acts 9:32-43; Kierkegaard (Purity of Heart)

DORCAS

Tabitha of Joppa, also called Dorcas
　　crafted in fabric with stitches:
an apron for grandma, a new dress for mom
　　and for brother some new denim britches.

She was gracious, precise and detailed,
　　generous to a fault and quite timely,
fitting and tatting, sewing and knitting,
　　serving her worshipping family.

Inspiring all others to higher perfection
　　she stitched on with nary an error.
Every fine detail utmost attention.
　　Excellence? She was the bearer!

The fair-linen cloth embroidered with crosses,
　　the veil and the burse, and the purificator.
The pall and the corporal, the frontal for altar,
　　she was their finest, their top fabricator.

The aim was to gain such artistic perfection
　　that no stitch or seam appear in the way.
What should be sensed is a mystical presence
　　a sacred impression of heavenly play.

The worshipper should feel support in devotion
　　not led aside by artistic pride.
Perfection in crafting is not the sought product
　　of flawless linen stitching.

A Red-shouldered Hawk

Should a worshipper take pause to admire her sewing,
    for Dorcas it would be just like breaking some law.
The item so crafted is not for attention,
    It is there for *without* it one might sense a flaw.

Jeremiah 20:7-13

COMPLIANCE

You got me into this and I Lord let you do it.
    You wore me to a frazzle so I now accede to you.
I'm a public joke, a mockery. Your word bugs me and it prods me;
    it's tormenting and it will not let me be.

If I try to just ignore it or forget it all completely,
    it's alive in all my bones and burns like fire in my gut,
a flame exploding in my belly and I cannot play the game.
    For my message is forever just the same:

Violence and death/destruction, ruination everywhere
    and the people think I'm nothing but a fool.
They're awaiting my undoing and are hoping that I'll stumble,
    looking for their chance to censure me for sure.

But you Lord are beside me. In the end I will be saved,
    their outrageous disrespect not overlooked.
You're God of hosts and you asses the righteousness of people,
    see the heart and mind and every soul's desire.

You are the judge and retribution is your province.
    And to you I have committed my whole cause.
Sing to the Lord with joyful noise and praise his holy presence.
    He delivers us from bandits and outlaws.

THE CHRISTMAS CROSS

He sent her a solid gold pectoral-cross
    all in a Christmassy spirit.
It was Black Hills gold with a neck chain
    and Yule-tide greetings went with it.

"Of all things," they pleaded, "a cross for her neck!
    Good grief man, how do you reason?
Would a crèche or a candle or angel work better,
    givin' the theme of the season?
'Tis a time of great joy, a time to make merry,
    the liturgical color is white!
Why send then a cross, a sign of Rome's gory,
    to celebrate *this* holy night?"

"According to legend," he countered,
    "the Black Hills are holy and valued.
The *Crazy Horse* monument attests to the faith.
    The land is both sacred and hallowed.
Gold from those hills must be steeped in that glory,
    most surely aflame in its light
There's no room for sadness, just joy, fun and gladness,
    faces all smiling and bright!"

    There is a hill called Golgotha
        where the holy cross was set.
    A hill of gloom and grief and death,
        of anguish, tears and fret.
    You're confusing your hills. One is of beauty,
        rich in its awesome magic.
    The other a trash-heap a dump beyond town,
        scavengers, rats, mostly tragic.

But our God is the Lord, Lord of redemption
    saving all that are broken and weak!
Then the lightening crashed and the thunder roared
    and I'm sure that I heard God speak:

    "I created those hills in Dakota, and hid that gold in the creek.
        And that land in the east, I created it too,
    the humble, the strong and the meek.
        I created it all and found it all good!
    A gift cross is not all that new
        Same as that cross on Golgotha hill,
        my sacrifice offered for you."

God does not reveal himself to us so that we can become preoccupied with religion, but in order that we might find meaning in life.
Martin Buber

CHRISTMAS BLESSINGS

He was righteous and deep, a true man of hope;
    the Spirit abided within him.
"You will see the Messiah before you pass on,"
    was the assurance that he had been given.

Just then in the Temple the child was presented.
    Simeon saw that his time now had come.
With the babe in his arms, he offered this praise,
    a song that's eternally sung:

"Master, your servant departs now in peace,
    having seen your salvation prepared before all.
A light for revelation for every nation
    and glory to your people throughout the hall."

Then he offered his blessing on all of them there
    as I herewith give mine to you:
God bless you and keep you in all that you do
and be your companion this whole New Year through.

Isaiah 11:1-9

THE MESSIANIC KING

He appears with the Spirit of God resting on him.
That Spirit is Wisdom, Counsel and Might,
the Spirit of Knowledge and Fear of the Lord.
Not one of Judgment but Understanding—Delight!

The poor and the meek all know his compassion.
The wicked have tripped on his fiery Word.
The gun on his hip he boldly calls, "Righteousness."
"Faithfulness," he labels the shells in his hoard.

The wolf, kid and leopard all bed down together.
The calf, bear and coyote browse one common meadow.
A child plays next to her pet cobra's den
and the lion eats corn like a mottled old hen.

There is no harm or destruction
on all of his Holy Mountain.
For the earth is as full of God's Glory
as is the sea with its eternal fountain.

O God, you make us glad by the yearly festival of the birth of your on-
ly Son Jesus Christ: Grant that we, who joyfully receive him as our redeemer,
may with sure confidence behold him when he comes to be our Judge; who
lives and reigns with you and the Holy Spirit, one God, now and forever,
Amen.
    (BCP)

SHALOM

Blessings to all from all of us here.
  Advent's now behind us, Epiphany's near.
Between them we're given twelve days of good cheer
    to then go forth in hope through a holy New Year.

PEACE is our prayer now for all the world's people.
  Hear it ring out aloud from every church steeple.
And peace be with you as we welcome the Son.
  May you journey with joy and outrageous good fun.

For to us:

A child is born; a son is given.
        He reins over all of creation.
His name is Amazing and Mighty;
        He is Eternal and Prince of Tranquility.

His domain is expanding without limitations
        bringing Shalom throughout all the nations,
enduring forever through all of our history!
        The zeal of the Lord guarantees us this mystery.

In the Sweet Gum Tree

Father in heaven:
          Holy is your name.
Your kingdom come,
Your will be done here,
          same as in heaven.
Give us our daily bread.
Forgive our sinning
          as we forgave others'
          sinning against us.
Keep us clear of temptation
and deliver us from evil.
                    The kingdom,
                    power and glory
                    are yours forever. Amen

I looked at the door one last time. The stare, which had been so intently on me for so long, now turned and looked to the side, following over his shoulder, as though watching someone pass through the door. And then he faded away. I took a deep breath and looked at the clock. It was exactly 7:00 a.m. I hadn't been certain that I was feeling Lynne's presence before that, but I was certain I felt the lack of it now.

Charlene's notes: Vigil 1/5/06

But yesterday, I fell back into the regular routine of early morning church work: helping with the altar, checking the lectionary, copying the bulletin. A few of us sat at the table folding those bulletins, enjoying again the quiet spirit of community, checking the details of the liturgy, when I had to look again. Sitting there, honoring the needs of my community and the time every minister devotes to it, it came to me. It is not Lynne's absence that remains, but her presence.

Meg Nichols' sermon: Memorial 1/9/06

PRESENCE

How does one feel without touch?
    How can one smell with no odor?
How does one see without light, hear with no vibes
    or taste where there is no flavor?
In short, how does one know the other is there
    if there is nothing at all there to savor?
Yet we do it quite well with almost no flare
    and with no discernible favor.

There is a mystical quality called *Presence*,
    a part of all sentient being,
detectable somehow through a "sixth sense"
    metaphorically referred to as feeling.
Nobody knows just why it should work,
    but most everyone testifies to it.
There is no special evidence the quality is real,
    but for the folk who are living life through it.

There is an attribute known as *Relationship*
    linking myriads of living things
in an arrangement known as Community
    made of many odd, tangled up rings.
The community can be measured and counted,
    and membership tracked over time.
But the "relationship" binding it can't be tallied or weighed
    and it's not merely crude or sublime.

So we have *Presence* whose presence is suspect,
    and *Relations* we can't prove are there.
Giving depth and rich fullness of meaning
    where meanings by right *should* prevail.
Yet they're mostly un-sensed by the standards of science
    nor in focus through our simple lenses.
Yes, there's more to reality than that range of substances
    detected by our common senses.

Thus to *be present* does not imply corporal reality,
    a spirit or ghost works just fine.
And *relationship* is not limited to nuclear families,
    it knits all of God's creatures through all of God's time.
So it is that the Christ who walks on the water
    and shows up in a padlocked room;
Is the one who forgives the people who slay him
    and who saunters away from his tomb.

So what can one say of reality?
    If it's not here is it there?
Is it really a matter of simple locality
    here or anywhere?
Could it be a function of faulty perception
    or of wild superstition and fear?
Is absence then truly a vacuum,
    nothing far off and empty up here?

Or does absence imply a removal
    to a different and unknown location?
Is it not really the same as *Being V void*
    in the Genesis account of creation?
Being is real because God's Word was spoken
    and being springs forth from the seal.
Who is to say what that Word should look like;
    if God already said it, then already it's real!

So much for *Presence*, now back to *Relationship*,
    linking all of us subjects together.
It is also called Love in most manifestations
    and the poets say love is forever.
Theologians assure us that Love is the Ultimate;
    in fact that it *is* what God *is*.
And Ultimate Reality is immeasurably broader
    than all that our senses take in.

So how can we doubt, something we "feel"
    such as a loved one's close proximity
on the basis of science, when science can't tell us
    just what love is definitively?
Now introduce faith,
    another decidedly unscientific term,
and add to that hope to complete
    good Saint Paul's eternally abiding trio.

So it's Faith, Hope and Love
    the cardinal virtues vying for consideration,
against see, hear and smell and the whole conglomerate
    of sensorial configuration.
I'm betting on Love, not Quantum Mechanics
    to save us from ultimate doom.
For Charlene and Meg it was not someone's theory
    but *Presence* they felt in the room.

TO: WESLEY FRENSDORFF

There once was a bishop named Wes
with whose humor we did not feel blessed
Then a cowpoke from Reno in a high-class casino
challenged to see who was best.
He was fast, he was slick; he had nerves of steel
as he reached for a spin of the wheel.
But he reeled, swayed and crashed,
he spun and he fell!
To the fastest pun in the west.

VALUING

She was loved, she was treasured, an important person.
    She was also a brazen, tenacious whore.
She was looked down on by the "people who counted."
    None tipped their hats nor left tips at the door.
They accepted her services in quiet gratitude
        then gossiped about her and went back for more.

Over the years she mothered three kids.
        Their names baldly taunted their mom's naked shame.
She was known just as Gomer, wife of Hosea
        and he truly loved her, notwithstanding her fame.
Hosea, by contrast, man of God in a mess,
        not of his liking but his just the same.

Insight is counted as one of God's Blessings.
        It seems to appear just when it is needed.
Such is the case in this bit of history.
        As Hosea pondered, wondered and pleaded
it eventually sunk in that his life was a parable
        of all that transpired from what had been seeded.

Hosea loved Gomer and he couldn't help it
        in spite of her faithless adultery and lusts.
As God loves all us in spite of our fervor
        for trinkets and trash and stuff that just rusts.
He desires our love not more gory rituals,
        our knowledge of him not more ashes and dust.

Value is set by who's doing the valuing.
    It is not a function of inherent worth,
and we are not worthy because of our value.
    We are first of all loved and in that is our worth.
By God and Hosea that lady was treasured
    and that's the way Gomer's value is measured.

COURSE ADJUSTMENT

There was a Manhattan business executive,
    who survived the Twin Towers disaster.
The Angel of Death he stared straight in the face,
    a terrifying, life-changing encounter.

Charlie had seen his whole life flash before him.
    What he had seen I can only surmise.
Confronted so suddenly he came to himself
    and arrived at this firm conviction:

"When I face this again, whatever the dread,
I want different images coursing through my head!"

He went back to his school and his studies
    determined to change his perspectives.
Vocation chose him, he completed the course
    and Charlie emerged a Registered Nurse.

In the Sweet Gum Tree

In 1987 Lynne made her Cursillo. This was my personal prayer of support.

PALANCA

From platitudes and tee shirt slogans
     shallow piety so unsure it must shout.
From suspicions or pious convictions that (X)
     is what anything is "all about, "
          Good Lord
              Deliver her?

From TV preachers and 'pop' theology,
     "Christian" athletes, authors and books,
bumper sticker religion and lack of vision,
     legalities and guilt trips with hooks,
          Good Lord
              Deliver her?

From plausible placebos and pabulum,
     from expositions (simplistic) of grace;
from clichés and assurances, and all "subtle nuances"
     (intended to help in the race),
          Good Lord
              Deliver her?
But,
let her glimpse the abyss with a shudder
     dread the truth of what she is seeing,
feel a chill in her spine, then turn to find
     your great love in the depths of her being.

Then,
to faith that embraces all doubting
     and to love that transcends the absurd;
to courage to accept your accepting,
     to encounter your fantastic Word,
          Good Lord
              Deliver her!

ON GIVING

Giving requires two parties to make it.
     A gift is no gift if the getter won't take it.
With getter compliance we're well on our way
     to happy sojourning and one pleasant day.

An item's a gift when the giver lets go.
     It's never a gift if the getter must owe.
As a thing is a gift as the giver turns loose,
     it can't be a gift when in truth it's a noose.

A gift is no gift if intent is control.
     Acquiring power can't be what gifts are for.
In fact, just the opposite's so it would seem.
     All folk should be free to both give and receive.

Expectation of thanks forfeits the gift's mission.
     Thanks is okay, its *expecting's* forfeiting.
Giver or getter might be the expector.
     Whatever! The gift's stamped REPAID in the *thanks for.*

Part of the joy shared in giving a gift
     is in seeing the getter receive it.
This point cancels out though if that's what the gift's for,
     for then the transaction is merely a barter.

If ever a phrase screamed for annihilation
     most surely *free gift* is that phrase.
For senseless redundancies formed to offend,
     "free gifts" grates on nerves like a curve on a bend.

Affection should find due expression in giving.
      An item's a gift when passed on with esteem.
It's hardly a gift if there's no love around it.
      The act needs regard on both ends of the dream.

The greatest gift ever's observed in December
      when we praise the Lord for his and remember!
The gift's wrapped in glory with his love unmatched
      and like every true gift, with no strings attached.

SAMSON'S RIDDLE

In the vineyards over at Timnah
    a lion threatened young Samson.
He threatened right back, grabbed hold of the cat
    and tore the great beast asunder.

Tossing it aside he continued his stride,
    romance was foremost on his mind.
He had found a fair maid in those vineyards,
    she was charming, yes quite a hot number.

    His desires were stirred, his passions afire;
    he was determined by thunder to have her!

No time to delay now, he wanted that girl now;
    libido was driving him blind.
He begged his folks urgently to get that foreign beauty
    for his matrimonial pleasure.

His desires were hot, his patience was not;
    the young stud sure needed corralling!
"But she is not of our kind; she's even left-handed,"
    his parents tried hard to fight back,

    "Show us a maid who will suite you,
    one from our own side of the track."

But Samson insisted; his parents caved in
    and they all took off for the city.
On the way, and aside,
    Samson checked out the remains

of the previously slaughtered kitty.
  To his surprise it was now a bee hive
all heavily laden with honey.
  He scooped out a treat for himself and his folks

  then, licking their fingers,
  went off to the party.

Guests had assembled, all set for a shoot-out,
  members of her tribe and kin
glaring at Samson and his obnoxious family
  as if they were little green men.

Then Samson, now trying to dispel all the tension,
  proposed a right-sporting riddle.
It was clan versus clan and the wager agreed then
  was a classy new wardrobe for all the men.

  They shook; the contest was on,
  and he put this puzzle to them:

      out of the eater, something to eat?
      out of the vicious, something sweet?

The guests had a week to come up with an answer
  as the celebration resumed without strife.
None had a clue to the sense of the riddle
  so they set out to pry it from Samson's new wife.

They wooed her, they teased her, and they pursued her
  with dogged persistence, eventually seduced her.
She was finally persuaded to betray her man.
  But he would have nothing to do with the plan.

"I have confided in no one, not even my parents,
why should I now explain it to you?

       The riddle's a secret. I will win the wager
       and put your family to shame."

Her nagging continued as did his resistance.
     Their vows could go hang in the rain.

"Two shall be one," was not so it seems,
     a promise impeding either one's means.
It was now a clan-feud not a marital-snit,
     a give-no-quarter in an all-out fit.

Then the day came; resolution was due.
     Two families lined up east and west.
Her folks, a little too confident declared:

       "A lion's the fieriest," says our money,
       and what could be sweeter than honey!"

With that Samson knew they had cheated.
     He cursed and he swore, he raged and he roared

       "Had you not plowed with my heifer
       you could never have ever resolved it!"

But the wager was lost and he had to make good.
     So he raided their warehouse at Ashkelon,
loaded a freight-car with festival garments
     and delivered the goods to their kin back at Timnah.

In this way his pride and also his bet-debt
     were simultaneously settled.
His best-man ran off with his discarded mate
     and Samson by now had a brand new hot date.

In the Sweet Gum Tree

Isaiah 35:5-10

THE HOLY WAY

Our eyes have been opened, our ears are unstopped,
mute tongues are singing for joy.
Here come the crippled, they're leaping like deer,
and rivers flow forth in the desert.

A highway is here, called GOD'S HOLY WAY.
It's here for God's Holy People.
Not even fools go astray on this Way.
No ravenous beast here may harm them.

The restored of the Lord have returned here today.
Endless Joy is here as our lever.
The Redeemed are enjoined to walk this hi-way
sighing and grieving are banned here forever.

Gracious Father, we pray for your holy Catholic Church. Fill it with all truth, in all truth with all peace. Where it is corrupt, purify it; where it is in error, direct it; where in anything it is amiss, reform it. Where it is right strengthen it; where it is in want, provide for it; where it is divided, reunite it; for the sake of Jesus Christ your son our savior. Amen
(BCP)

SHEPHERD OF TEKOA

The day of the Lord is not what you think,
    it's not all peaches and cream.
It's darkness, not light as you like to dream,
    gloom enough to make anyone scream.

Like you flee from a wolf on the side of a hill
    into the claws of a bear in the valley below.
Or dash into the cabin to avoid a live scorpion
    and run into a rattler coiled up on the floor.

Skip your High Masses and quaint celebrations,
    I take no delight in your festival feasts.
Never mind your *Hail Marys* and your *God Bless Americas*.
    I am not impressed by your over-fed beasts.

Your sonorous organ-swells bore me enormously;
    Alleluias and *Praise Jesuses* I can well do without.
The um-pas and whining of expensive instruments
    get you no Brownie points, earn you no clout.

Those harmonious renderings I will not attend to,
    not noise, stunts or dancing or a thing you can sing.
But let justice roll down like Niagara Falls
    and righteousness rage like floodwaters in Spring.

ANANIAS' MISSION

A disciple of Damascus, one devout Ananias
    was called by the Lord in a vision.
He was told to go see a rebellious church wrecker,
    a guy known as Saul and a strict Pharisee.

Ananias was dubious. He knew who this guy was;
    to meet him did not seem that prudent.
He was dragging his feet but the Lord was insistent;
    the Spirit pressed on and could not be resisted.

He found Saul as ordered, blind as a bat,
    prayerful, repentant, subdued and all that.
He was even expecting this messenger's call
    who then shouted out to him, "Hey, Brother Saul!

"The Lord Jesus who struck you and got your attention
    while you were en-route to our town
has sent me to show you the way you must travel.
    From here on this is the road you will go on."

He laid hands upon him, the lights all went up.
    Eyesight and insight hit Saul in a flash.
He was now an Apostle, zeal still like a rod,
    converted, baptized in the service of God.

67

RELUCTANT PROPHET

The seafarers were an uneasy lot,
      wary as a ship's crew could be,
with cause to suppose that their god was opposed
      to their perilous plot on the sea.

How else to explain the threatening winds
      and the wild and foreboding waves
now plaguing their trip, threatening their ship
      and calling forth all of that rage.

So they scattered the bones and checked out the stars
      seeking an explanation.
Their plight was no mystery. But *why?* was the question!
      Because of somebody's transgression?

The lot fell on Jonah, a mysterious traveler
      on a quest not obvious to them.
Then fast asleep in the hold down below
      oblivious to their dawning doubts about him.

He was out to escape the Lord's clear command
      to take on a mission in Syria.
A summons to preach, "repentance or else!"
      to the decadent people of Nineveh.

Rejecting this call, he had tried to take off
      for some far-away land not to mention.
Saying "No!" to a call, doesn't sit well with God
      who at least had the sailors' attention.

In the Sweet Gum Tree

So they threw Jonah off, kicking and screaming,
        where a whale of a fish picked him up,
took him to his home port for one other take
        on the Lord's afore-mentioned commission.

Jonah meanly agreed though he also was sure
        that Yahweh's most merciful proclivities
would severely impair *his* planned revenge
        on Nineveh's rebellious and immoral citizens.

Jonah got to the city, opened up a store-front
        and launched his street-preaching campaign.
His spirit was in it, the message took hold
        exactly as he had expected.

They flocked to Confession in sackcloth and ashes
        and prayed for the Lord's kind compassion.
They were repentant, contrite - lowly miserable sinners -
        now eager to set things anew and upright.

Jonah knew he could do it but not why he should;
        these sinners just didn't deserve it.
What's wrong with revenge when the jerks have it coming?
        Is not *Justice* just what we are after?

But the Lord changed his mind and would not follow through
        exactly as Jonah predicted.
He was fit to be tied, disgusted with God;
        his thirst for revenge not now to be sated.

But, mission complete, the people converted.
        How does a successful seer top that?
Shut down the store-front, slip out of town,
        then find a convenient locale for observing!

So Jonah sat down on the outskirts of town
      just to see what might take place next.
God had saved a great city (with Jonah's assistance?)
      how now to wrap up that in context?

The site picked for viewing was open and sunny;
      in fact it was downright sizzling.
God appointed a bush to grow there and shade him,
      effective relief from the grilling.

Jonah sat in the shade with a gentle breeze stirring
      all through the rest of the day.
Then God sent a worm that girdled that bush
      so it dried up and withered away.

Jonah sat there complaining; he wished he were dead.
      He was not a happy camper.
It was God's turn to preach so he squared off to teach
      his complaining, reluctant companion.

"You pity a bush that lived but one day
      but think that those people don't matter.
Yet, we have just saved many thousands of souls,
      plus all of their donkeys and cattle."

ELECTRONIC CHAOS

Dark Matter so they tell me can't be seen, touched or heard.
    It really isn't questioned though its presence is "inferred."
A Black Hole, on the other hand, a raving, hungry beast;
    any matter crossing over, just another tasty feast.

The boundary separating this domain from something other
    is an Event Horizon; NO TRESPASSING signs all over.
Nobody knows what lies beyond that scary, daunting border.
    Pass over it, you're past the reach of any kind of order.

A Little Stroll through Space could be a book for *Hawking's* crafting.
    It might help me to understand the universe so baffling.
Till then I guess I'll just get by with this initial finding.
    (The topic's surely *Stephen's,* so my findings can't be binding.)

The Black Hole, sure enough is here; it lurks in my computer.
    It gobbles up without a trace all data I can feed'er.
The Event Horizon guarding its domain and messy hoard
    is crawling in the gaps and cracks of this be-damned keyboard.

71

PROPHET OF MORESHETH

Stand up and plead your argument
    before the Rocky Mountains.
Shout out from the Grand Tetons
    to the Appalachian Range.

The Lord files this complaint against
    rebellious, errant people
from the lofty hills and valleys,
    through the broad and rolling plains.

"I saved you from the British twice
    as you were getting started.
I saved you from yourselves again
    in civil warfare parted.

"I raised you to a super-state
    when countries cried for help.
I made you a redeeming force
    while nations brawled and battled.

"But what about your part in
    this blessed, holy contract?
You lie and rape and cheat and steal
    right here with one another.

"Your rich are bent on getting more,
    no matter who gets trampled.
While poor just keep on losing ground
    and justice doesn't matter.

In the Sweet Gum Tree

"But why with all of your feasting
        is your hunger never sated?
And why with profit's steady flow
        does debt as steadily still grow?

"And with all your frantic sowing
        where is commensurate reaping?
Given all the anxious trampling,
        where's the olive oil and wine?"

What is it then that God demands,
        more yearlings on the altar?
Maybe more than ten thousand more
        dimes in the bell ringer's coffer?

Does he want all my wealth, my worldly treasure,
        my home and all my belongings?
My name and the legends I have acquired,
        the respect that I have commanded?

I regularly donate and contribute my time
        to the Elks' and Lions' causes.
I attend church some, yes, now and then
        and have even sung in the chorus.

So, what is expected of a middle class guy?
        my firstborn, my own flesh and blood?
The fruit of my loins for my sin and my crud?
        I am not all that rich and I'm sure not on fire!

He has already told you what is required:
        it is justice and kindness in a spirit of love.
Not tentative stumbling down some rutted road
        and not your feet that just plod.

It's your heart and your soul and your being
  in sync with what's Ultimately Real,
your humble and steadfast walk
  in the Spirit and Way of your God.

Ecclesiasticus 43:1-12, 27-32

PRIDE OF THE REALMS

The vault of the sky is the pride of the realms
     and a glory to see; our view of the blue.
The sun is advising in its very rising
     what a marvelous instrument it truly is.

It parches the land like a fiery furnace.
     Who is alive in its scorching heat?
It burns up the mountain and breathes fiery wrath;
     its rays blind the eyes as it moves down its path.

The moon marks the time of the change of the seasons,
     a beacon to hosts in the dome of the sky!
Governing the times for the festival replays,
     renewing itself in incomparable displays.

The stars can't escape their custodial duty,
     a glittering array in the heights of the Lord.
And the rainbow encircles the sky in an arc
     spectacular as fireworks viewed in the park.

OFFERATORY

In this offering we are making
        are our lives and how they went,
on our play and on our work,
        with our time and our intent.

All of self we have expended
        since the last such an event
a treasure of our stewardship,
        affirmation we've been sent.

It's no tithe, it's not a portion,
        not a share of gifts received.
It's no sacrifice or debt paid;
        it's our **gift,** be not deceived.

THE SENTINEL
A RED-SHOULDERED HAWK
IN THE SWEET GUM TREE

There's an old dead stem of a sweet gum tree
    out over the inlet across from me.
Through my back glass door quite easy to see,
    just the forty foot trunk of an old dead tree.

Not a leaf or a twig in my view remains;
    naked and gaunt this old stick reigns.
Not many more seasons can it stay that way
    then there'll be no tree to pervade my day.

Perched up high in this dead old stem
    a red-shouldered hawk inspecting the glen.
Like a sentinel guarding the vale below
    eyeing small creatures as they come and go.

Far to the east in the bright blue sky,
    the trail of a jet-plane flying high.
A white chalk line there a'tracing north
    its appointed course as it journeys forth.

Could it be that the hawk sees that line too?
`   A vapor trail through a field of blue?
Then wonders what sort of a critter that be
    leaves a scent-free trail so easy to see?

Ah, the mysteries of life haunt this soul too:
    why we are here and what we should do?
Is there meaning in life then, when it's all said,
    with the green leaves gone and the twigs all dead?

77

The chalk trail fades from the sky's clear blue.
      The plane's still there, but now lost to view.
Still traveling north, its appointed race
      expecting to be welcomed at its own home base.

Is there some super-hawk eying our faint trails,
      redeeming our treks and our muffled wails?
While we travel on attending to a call
      toward a paradise known long before our fall?

What's the grand old stem of a sweet gum tree
      or a white chalk line in a sky of blue
have ever to do with me or with you,
      as we press our course as we're bound to do?

We never came to be or to find our niche
      through our own design or a plan of our own pick.
And we'll keep on going as we're called to roam
      till the mission is completed and we're welcomed home!

Psalm 121

THE WAGON MASTER

Look to the hills. See, our sentries are posted,
      each one assigned a strategic position.
The kids are tucked in and already asleep;
      let us pray our defenses are working.
By sticking together we pool our protection
      but bandits in darkness are everywhere lurking.

We came here from places all over the realm
      for our mandated journey to Zion.
It's a duty you see for each one of us here
      at least once in our personal history,
to worship the Lord in Jerusalem
      in the Temple in God's Holy Mystery.

We have kept all our wagons together
      believing there's safety in numbers.
Just one wagon train for maximum gain
      and our leader, a skilled Wagon Master.
Our real hope however is our trust in the Lord,
      our Savior and Heavenly Pastor.

It is he who will watch and he will assure
      that our feet are secure and that we do not stumble.
And unlike our sentries, *his* eyes will not droop;
      he won't fall asleep and will never slumber.
It's the Lord keeping watch through the light of the day
      who shades us from sun's scorching heat.

And our God will keep guard through the dangers of night
        protecting from all lunar evils.
The mind works strange tricks under cover of dark
        and our journey continues tomorrow.
But, destination is nearer than when we began.
        So far we have seen little sorrow.

So we look to the hills where our sentries are posted,
        but press on ahead in our Father's keep.
The kids run and skip with no sense at all
        of the dangers as we galloped faster.
Our mission complete now, our wagons are safe now
        by grace of our God, the True Wagon Master.

Psalm 139:6-11

DARKNESS BANISHED

From the heights of heaven to the depths of the sea
      you were there in their joy when my parents conceived me.
To the quiet of the grave where they laid me to rest
      your Spirit is with me, your hands hold me blest.

The darkness is never a darkness to you.
      The night is as bright as the daylight.
Darkness and light are to you both alike.
      At all times, in all places your Presence *is* light.

RECYCLING

That grand old trunk of a Sweet Gum tree, stark in the sky of blue
has succumbed to violent wind and rain, to age and to morning dew.
It no longer reigns as a sentinel bold out back and within my view,
downed as was destined years ago since it grew up there brand new.

But the story isn't over of the Sweet Gum's daunting theme
that once brightened up my hour, entertained my pleasant dream.
It has sheltered cheerful song birds and encouraged squirrels' play,
given vantage to the hawk and owl and pleasure to my day.

That legend I'm relating likely ran a hundred years,
from seedling's slender, tender start in tenuous seedling fears.
Through season after season of enduring weather's jeers
while growing strong and gaining bulk, a bulwark without peers.

Till its foliage was destroyed and the tree no longer breathed,
Life-giving sap no longer coursed and all the forest grieved.
Yet it stood there stark and bold and high still reaching for the sky.
Its grandeur not diminished and its witness not to die.

May the Lord in loving mercy give us all such graceful byes
to witness Truth and Faith and Love far after our demise!
To stand up strong midst ravages of storm and lightning strikes
and not succumb to taunts or jeers or gossip's bitter bites.

In the Sweet Gum Tree

In shade of that old rotting log and decomposing blight
a slender new twig sprouts there and is reaching for the light.
A Live Oak sapling growing now well rooted in the bog
set well enough right now to reach up high into the fog.

I am thinking of my lover who succumbed before her time
to the ravages of cancer, ruthless killer by design.
How I miss her boisterous laughter and the joy she brought my way,
so spontaneous, exciting and as free as children's play.

Yet her mission isn't over and her witness still bears leaves.
The life that once coursed through her veins now livens others' dreams.
New ventures she once dreamed of are alive and sing her song
like a Live Oak springing from the bog, new life cannot be wrong.

We call it resurrection and confess to ever seeing
that a living soul embraced in love just doesn't give up being.
The tree may die but treeness simply does not go away.
In song and verse, in forests that idea's here to stay.

Truth and faith and love, and life itself are likewise ever with us.
Not to feel or taste or smell or weigh, their properties elude us.
But precious, every one of them if never tracked by senses.
Their being is not doubted and their value never ended.

So in essence and transcendence nothing true or loved is gone.
Not the Sweet Gum tree, the hawk or owl, or the one for whom I long.
The qualities, the truths, the loves of yours and mine and ours
are sprouting fresh and new out there with all the other flowers.

A Red-shouldered Hawk

Matthew 25:31-46

THE GREAT JUDGMENT

When he appears in his ravishing glory
    surrounded by thousands of seraphim,
when seating himself on the uppermost story
    all nations assembled below and before him,

He'll divide all those folk to his right and his left
    and solemnly make final judgment upon them.
To those on his right, "Welcome, join me up here
    for you are the blessed of the Lord, never fear.

"Here is the place where you all now may hang,
    made ready for you since creation's big-bang.
For, when I near starved you gave bread I could eat,
    when thirsty you gave me cold water to drink.

"As outcast you welcomed me into your flat.
    When naked you gave me a robe for my back.
I was sick; you anointed my sores and my scars.
    Locked-up, you embraced me through cold iron bars."

Then will the blessed bewildered respond,
    "Sir, when could that be that we tended thee,
saw you were starved and put food on your plate?
    Or thirsty and gave you cool water to sate?

"And Sir whenever could it have ever been so,
    that as a stranger we greeted you, 'Lo,
Peace and please enter. You're welcome, Hello!
    How are you? Good health, and Pour you some jo?'

"Or seeing you naked grabbed clothes from our rack
     and gave you a shirt or a robe for your back?
And whenever could it have ever been thus
     that we found you ailing and nursed you and such.

"Or in prison and paid you a pastoral call?"
     And the king will say, "Truly, I'm telling you all
as sure as you did it for any of these,
     all members of my earthly clan, if you please,

"most surely indeed, so you did it for me!"
     Then, turning to those on his left he'll decree,
"Scram! Get on out of here. You can't be free!
     You're destined for hell as you already see!

"And hell's prepared too, all ready for all you.
     For, when I was hungry you gave me no food.
When thirsty you gave me no water to drink;
     an outcast you left me adrift just to sink.

"When naked ne'r bothered to cover my pride,
     when sick or in prison cared zip for my hide."
Then they too will answer, "Lord, just when was that,
     that we saw you hungry or thirsty, estranged?

"Or naked, imprisoned and utterly failed you,
     to see to your needs? Lord, just when was that?"
Then he will come back, "Oh man, you don't get it.
     You never saw fit to help any poor slob,

"much less be a friend to some tramp in your village,
     see! You discounted me. It's not complicated!"
And these will be cast into darkest extinction,
     the righteous be saved for most blessed distinction.

PENTECOST

The big day arrives with the delegates here
      in one massive hall on the east side of town.
While outside the flags of dozens of nations
      wave proudly aloft from their poles in the round.

Inside the Chair keeps on pounding the lectern
      trying to get them all quieted down.
The horde however, unruly as ever
      continues their fighting, quietened never.

Conceding defeat, a frustrated Chair
      flings her notations all over the ground.
No surprise that, seeing those who are there.
      It's a Tower of Babel and all of them blubbering.

Arabs and Russians, Armenians and Jews,
      Italians and Germans and Turks all a-muttering.
Asians, Australians, black folk and white;
      none can make out what another is uttering.

Confusion in multiples of sevens and eights,
      utter chaos with everyone chatting and sputtering.
Then suddenly from nowhere we feel a strong presence,
      it roars through the manor with hurricane force.

Scorching everyone present, a brushfire in essence,
      inspiring each with a new kind of speech.
Then everyone here understands quite precisely
      just what all the others are trying to preach.

The Tower of Babel is now in reverse,
      incoherent to some, (in tongues they were praying)
comprehended by all in ways strangely diverse.
      Then Peter speaks up facing all those assembled,

"You obviously think that these people are plastered.
      But it's nine in the morn, not likely a binge.
What you have witnessed, divisiveness mastered."
      It was Joel who forewarned us the Spirit would come,

"'Infusing with power all flesh," so he raved
      with visions and dreams and wisdom prophetic.
"Who calls on the Lord will surely be saved."
      So also David witnessed about him,

"I'm glad, I rejoice, he is at my right hand.
      I will not be rattled but live on in faith.
He won't abandon nor bring me corruption.
      He's granted me life and his presence is grace."

Then tongues of fire (like Liberty's torch)
      alight upon every last one of us here.
Bells start their clanging, they scream out in fear.
      Engines deploy, it's completely chaotic.

Saint Peter attempts to assure us once more,
      "This is not a madness, Spirit is here!
This Jesus you crucified is our Messiah.
      He was raised and now we have seen it.

"Being therefore exulted at God's own right hand
      we've received his own promise of Spirit.
He has poured out on us as you both see and hear."
      Folk scramble for shelter, disaster is near.

A Red-shouldered Hawk

While outside the flags of dozens of nations
        wave proudly aloft from their poles in the round.
We are touched to the quick, "Which way do we go?"
        "Repent, be baptized, in the name of the Lord.

"You are free and your sins are forgiven."
        Three thousand new members are added right here,
making the church their new home.
        Committing themselves immediately

to the Apostles' communion and creed,
        to the breaking of bread and the prayers
as the church flames like fire
        and God's people are freed.

Great news here and now for all People of God,
        but some folk are not good at hearing.
Thus, everyone present is given a chance to
        rethink what so many are fearing.

But the world doesn't notice; it's business as usual
        as wars wage on all around.
And outside the flags of dozens of nations
        droop sadly and limp from their posts in the ground.

Isaiah 49:6-7

Hey, it's no great hurrah, nothing really oh man
        that you, my appointed, should save just one clan.
I called you to be as a light to all nations,
        that good news be spread to the ends of the earth.
Kings will salute you and princes bow down
        in the name of the Lord you've been given new birth.

MEANS THAT DELIGHT
A TELEOLOGICAL OPTION

Who made up the rule that the purpose comes first
and determines the course of the action?
Why not see initially the action kick-off
then purpose can find its place after?

A cause is assumed to precede the effect
and create the effect's unique traits.
Why can't we see first the result and its specs
then up and create a responsible launcher?

Results, we are told, can't be first on the scene,
there must first be a triggering reason.
Why not just approve the result in advance
and then fabricate an accountable trigger?

Why couldn't there be a signal out front
compelling us all toward bold, daring action?
Without specifying outcomes and results
or even recounting each minute infraction?

Who said that the end must justify means?
That sequence is sure not divine.
Let's challenge that order at least this one time:
Choose means that delight, results could be fine!

TIME AND ETERNITY
CLOCKS 'N STUFF

I never had a digital watch
    and don't ever expect to have one.
It's what they imply of the nature of time
    and how they abuse the time that is mine.

Digitals don't share with us minutes or hours. They
    just keep on flashing their "now," "now" and "now!"
They give us no sense of before or hereafter
    insistently blinking their no-time but "now."

An hour glass gives us a feel for enduring,
    the sand in the top is the future still due.
That down below is time no longer new
    while the stuff in between? Just passing through!

There's no way to stop it or even to see it.
    An elusive event evading our greeting
from a future entirely out of our reach
    to a past that is gone and keeps on receding.

So "now" in finality has no reality.
    It's a slippery transition that we cannot measure
between those two "times" beyond our experience,
    a flirtatious and virtual un-appearance.

Then we have clocks with their wide sweeping hands
    covering all of our temporal places.
They do not flash digits or filter fine grains,
    just point timely fingers at figures on faces.

So, here is a digital claiming no time but now.
    An hour glass saying that now's an illusion.
While clocks are insisting, "it just doesn't matter,
    it'll come back around again in profusion."

But what do we mean by "before" and "hereafter,"
    "enduring" and "waiting" and "just killing time?"
What is time anyway? Where is the treasure
    if there's nothing at all there to weigh in or measure?

We know that we cannot induce it
    to slow down, to pause or to go any faster.
Time is a "relative," it's not our domain
    to create it, erase it or behave like its master.

We have no control; it's all on its own.
    We cannot put time on display.
We can save it or waste it or sell it or kill it
    but what *it* is we can't really say!

Places make spaces to claim their reality.
    They can be positioned right there on the chart,
perhaps on a mountain or in a valley,
    at a crossroads or bridge, at a dam or a port.

Dates too can claim their share of the fame
    but are not given places on sea-charts or lanes.
The place might provide an event with a name
    but timing no doubt still counts just the same.

They tell us that time truly had a beginning
    when all of creation got started.
We are not in position to acclaim or deplore
    anything about there, then or before.

So time was created. That much seems sure.
      Events invent patience so acts can endure;
things make up spaces for stuff to exist in.
      Thus action plus stuff is creation persisting.

So now time and space are two of the givin's.
      They are not "created," they are the context.
We are constrained to life played on this stage.
      The story continues now page after page.

But if you still wonder, consider just this:
      before time began out there in the mist
it was void, empty, vacant, so utterly nothing
      the notion of *was* didn't even exist.

That takes us back some fourteen billion years,
      an incredible number for us to fathom
measured in units of time, don't you know,
      units of "time" not just units at random.

But suppose we could see out beyond the horizon
      exceeding the bounds of all times and all places,
no digitals or clocks there proclaiming authority
      for our cautious moves nor the glow in our faces.

Out there in the midst twixt orbits and spheres,
      beyond time and accounting for minutes or years,
all gear and all actions, all crafters unfurling,
      the span of all things and all tragic occurring

to a totally different and glorious reality
      transcending this whole scheme of actions and stuff,
affirming and healing and blessing creation, yet
      ultimate in Meaning and Being for us.

NOMENCLATURE

The greatest sin ever is tagging a brother
    with labels that say, "You're not in."
Yet we do it with such regularity
    that we don't recognize it as sin.

One can't be a *visitor* in God's holy house.
    One's never a *guest* in one's own father's home.
Tourist, sightseer, visitor and *guest* are labels
    for all those we don't claim our own.

Not labels that say *hey, this one is in*
    but labels that tell us that *this one is out.*
New faces among us are God's children, so
    there's no one among us whom God doesn't know.

We are People of God and not really rare.
    Call us *sisters* or *brothers* or . . . *children* is fair.
We are also called *members* as in "parts of a body."
    A member's alive and is corporally there.

Like a hand or a foot is a member of me.
    It shares in my feelings and intimate dealings.
A term used by Paul who also used saints,
    so we're *saints* or we're *members*, not visitors, we.

Collectively known as *Community* or *Church*,
    Parish or *Mission*, that also works.
Congregation or *Family*? Those too are fair,
    but not bunch or gang or just them over there.

A Red-shouldered Hawk

We are not subdivided by status or classes;
       once duly baptized one's a member, that's it!
If one's not on the roster, then throw out that list
       not the brother or sister, the list won't be missed.

Why should we welcome those who belong here?
       Why should we pose like we are the host?
How presumptuous of us to play compere
       when all of us here by rights should feel home free?

This is God's holy temple; God is the host.
       We are all of us home in our father's mansion.
We have not stopped to just pay our respects
       we are here at our Lord's invitation.

A gathering of members not gaggle of guests,
       meeting to praise him and hear his Word read,
to share in baptizing and breaking of bread,
       a part of his body, who arose from the dead.

PATIENCE

I praise you dear Lord for all people's patience.
　　Without it how would we old timers get by?
I thank you for sisters and brothers and cousins
　　and all family members who give it a try.

I thank you for strangers in line at the counter
　　who don't shake their watches or yawn or complain,
but quietly wait while I awkwardly balance
　　with hand in my pocket, my wallet and cane.

I thank you for neighbors and their smiling faces
　　as my slowing gait ties up their parking places.
I thank you for friends and for their calm excuses
　　when they let it go as my hearing reduces.

I thank you for others who see I am rushing
　　though my pace is now much like that of a snail.
I thank you for drivers who yield right-of-way
　　when I take the wrong lane and foul up their day.

And thanks Lord for children, especially mine.
　　I once changed their diapers and taught them what's fine.
Now they give me spaces where I don t belong
　　and steady my pace as I shuffle along.

A Red-shouldered Hawk

I Corinthians 12:27-14:1

MINISTRY
PAUL'S MANUAL

We are prophets and healers and speakers in tongues,
       rulers and singers and beaters of drums.
We are parts of one body, varieties of roles
       according to gifts with which each is bestowed.

Yet there's no call for boasting on anyone's part
       because of some ranking of gifts or gift's art.
They are GIFTS, don't you know. We didn't invent them.
       Nor were we told which apostles should get them.

Cease all that bragging and stupid upstaging.
       No one gets all gifts but we are all still one.
So listen up now to what I have to say,
       there is to be sure a more excellent way.

If I speak in the tongues of mortals or angels
       yet not speak in love I'm just rattling cages.
Give me all preaching powers and deep spiritual fountains,
       the knowledge of scholars and faith to move mountains.

Yet still with no love I am nothing at all!
       I could give all I've got to feed hungry people,
even my life to save some beggar's neck.
       And so, I might boast but if love is not in it

not a pittance accrues to this mortal's credit.
       With no love there is nothing there for me to claim.
Even sinners go trading while gaining no blame.
       So, what's it to us doing merely the same?

In the Sweet Gum Tree

Love is for sure love's own collateral,
	patient and kind, rejoicing in truth.
It's not ever arrogant, envious or boastful,
	irritable, resentful, churlish nor rude.

Love bears up with joy the weight of it all,
	believes and endures in spite of it all,
maintains hope and cheer through the thick of it all
	and love never quits but stands firm and tall!

Our preaching will someday fade out and yes, cease.
	Tongues too, will retire from their wagging and quit.
Not even our knowledge will then still persist.
	All will come to a close and so finally desist.

For our knowledge and vision and prophetic insight,
	so fragile, so partial, so doomed to take flight.
When that which is thorough responds to his call
	these fragments will then count for nothing at all.

When I was a child, I talked like a child.
	I thought and I reasoned just like a child.
But now I'm adult, time to end childish ways,
	a new actuality, new times, no delays.

For now we see only as in a fogged mirror,
	but then we'll see clearly, as true face to face.
Now I know only in pieces and bits,
	then I'll know fully, as so fully I'm known.

For now we have faith, hope and love, yes, all three,
	and love is the greatest gift there'll ever be.
We're grateful for all gifts that bless you and me.
	But love is the essence of all ministry.

ONTOLOGICAL REALITY

Fundamentally love is a state of being, the prime ontological reality.
    This truth must be grasped and enjoyed with tenacity
if one is to fathom one's daily experience
    of existential expressions of essential veracity.

Love's expressions shine forth in emotions and actions
    like a couple confessing their feelings and passions
or admitting their mutual love-making pro-actions.
    It's beyond their control and for now is not rationed.

So love *is*, as in being, and Love acts, as in doing.
    Love claims both conditions are so.
Just ask any lover and you will discover
    they have found it is factual with one another.

It is out of this world, it is blessed by our Lord;
    it has been given for the Eternal.
So come on in now by twos, threes or fours;
    entry's forbidden a loner.

The Reality Love abides with two sisters;
    the three are functionally one. One sister's called Justice,
the other one Force; each sister is slighted if courted alone.
    In essence they're inter-dependent.

So, it's Love, Force and Justice, a single reality;
    the three must be treated as one.
Take care to recall one alone doesn't get it
    and if one of three's missing the sense is undone.

In Love without Justice anything goes.
    Love without Force has no hooks.
Force by itself is all power with no purpose where
    Justice alone is mere balancing books.

Love and Force as a team is sweet, sticky drivel
    with hardly responsible character.
Love with Justice together sound nice it is true,
    abstract pious wishes with nothing to do.

Power with Justice is Virtue on steroids
    but whatever happened to care?
It's the triad in balance we're seeking;
    Love minus her kin is a weakling.

Love as in this triad is God's Love on earth.
    John says, "It's the Being that God truly Is."
No peaches and cream indiscriminately;
    no forget it, my child, through infinity!

Love is not toothless, carefree or stupid
    but Love is the final Redeemer.
Each sis understands she's not lost in the union
    for then would the triad be *only* a union.

Each self, it is known, cannot stand there alone'
    in that, love is simply potential.
Three sisters together comprise this normality;
    it's the Prime Ontological Reality.

SOWING SEED

He sits in the boat, dodging curious masses
    crowding and shoving all over the beach.
Holds one hand up high, waves to them to heed
    while he speaks of carelessly broadcasting seed.

Some seed it seems falls there twixt the flagstones,
    some falls directly onto the path.
Other is scattered on the edge of the walkway
    midst brambles and weeds and stray stands of hay.

Some actually ends up in moist, sandy loam
    ideal for any seed seeking a home.
"But what is his point?" The crowd is bewildered.
    This can't be a course on how wheat fields are sown.

Too costly and wasteful, who'd pay such a price?
    Pointless investment, ridiculous advice!
Sparrows consume the seed on the trail,
    weeds choke any that sprout by the rail.

The only seed having a modicum of chance
    is that grain that lands in prepared sandy loam.
Sparrows or chickens will get most of what's scattered.
    Terrible extravagance! Thrift just doesn't matter.

The crowds are spellbound as he holds their attention
    with all of that talk, wasting all of that seed!
"But what is his point?" Repeating the question,
    bemused but still awed by his audacious creed.

He's speaking in parables, that much seems clear.
    But that doesn't help us decipher the code.
The boat now is rocking, the crowd pressing closer.
    Can't stand up for emphasis, risk swamping the load!

So he sits there admonishing, "Have you no ears?
    Open your eyes, hear and perceive.
Your heart has grown dull, your mind no longer keen.
    But those who have now, even more they'll receive."

A youngster is wading up over his knees,
    listening intently, hair roughed in the breeze.
"I got it!" he yells out, "He speaks of his kingdom
    and we are all welcome, though not fit for seeds.

"He's spreading his Word through all nooks and crannies
    with most of it falling on unfitted ears.
He willingly offers his body and blood here
    and his grace defuses everyone's fears."

The sermon continues while listeners crowd closer.
    "Converting the crowds is what we are after.
Yet every seed's valued by he who is sowing
    and any seed *might* sprout in soil fit for growing."

But they still don't get it, their senses can't help.
    "Prophets have longed for just what you see."
While they are attuned to some odd minor key.
    "If I could touch their cold hearts I could set them free!"

The crowd starts dispersing, interest is waning.
    Some guy caught a big one, far side of the lake.
A large-mouth bass or another big bull-head?
    Could be a contender for this season's take.

A youngster is wading up over his knees,
    listening intently, hair roughed in the breeze.
Eyes and ears totally tuned to essentials
    but who honors a kid who has no credentials?

James 1:11-18

BLESSED ENDURANCE

Temptation and lure do not come from God.
    They are rooted in our own desire.
Then desire conceives and gives birth to sin
    and what sin in maturity gives birth to is dire.

Generosity, beloved is what comes from above,
    conceived by the father of lights.
It was he gave us birth by his word of truth
    that we be his topmost desire.

Blessed are you who have withstood the test.
    You were lured and yet stayed with the best.
Now you've received the crown of life promised
    to all of those people who love without rest.

A Red-shouldered Hawk

VOCATION

If satisfaction is there in the action
　　and talent is taxed on the way;
if the process delights and enlightens the ride
　　and the product gives rise to deep personal pride,
then you, my dear friend are not working at all.
　　You are, most assuredly heeding your call!

If the action is but a detraction
　　and talent not stretched on the way,
Ii the procedures don't hold the attention
　　and the product not worthy of mention
then beware my good friend, you are wasting your mind
　　and the position you're filling is naught but a grind!

Matthew 6:19-21

*Lay not up for yourself treasures on earth where moth and rust doth corrupt
and thieves break through and steal.
But lay up for yourself treasure in heaven where neither moth nor rust doth
corrupt nor thieves break through and steal.
For where your treasure is there will your heart be also.*

1 Kings 22:1-38

MICAIAH

The kings of Israel and Judah one day
      stretched out on their posh royal thrones,
were enjoying their afternoon tea time
      while relaxing their weary old bones.

They were there at the fortified, main city gates
      of that glorious metropolis Samaria,
clad in their finest of purple and gold,
      the center of attraction, a sight to behold.

The prophets meanwhile were prancing about,
      playing regally adroit and proficient
while casting their lots and tossing their dice,
      reading their tea leaves and betting their ice.

Along about four regal languor crept in
      as the monarch of Israel, refilling his cup,
proposed this inane and plain childish plan,
      "Let's up and make war on the King of Aram!

"I've a long standing land claim right there on his turf."
      Jehoshaphat was willing though not to be rushed.
"But first we just really must check with the seers.
      A nod from the prophets would calm people's fears."

"Oh, they're in my pocket, on my side already.
      Behold how they're now out there carrying on.
That's all for me - I put jam on their toast!
      They just wouldn't dare disagree on a boast."

105

A little bit dubious, Jehoshaphat waffled.
    "But shouldn't we look for a second opinion?
Is there some other voice that perhaps we should heed?
    Is that not the way cautious kings should proceed?"

So they summoned Micaiah, the radical seer,
    predictable critic of all of his peers.
While his word was bound to unsettle the plot,
    due process demanded they give it a shot.

Micaiah was warned right up front by his callers,
    advised to agree with inferior colleagues.
The seer came by there and playing the dunce
    put forth all the drivel they wanted at once.

"Go up and attack Ramouth Gilead.
    The Lord has given it over to you,
like taking candy away from a babe.
    Just scurry on up there and don't be afraid."

The king was no fool and he snapped right back,
    "Haven't I warned you time and again
when I ask for your counsel just give me straight dope,
    no light-hearted joking or fool-hardy hope.

"I fully expect of you word of the Lord.
    Just give me clear counsel directly from him,
a serious critique of our planned course of action."
    Micaiah, responded now solemn and grim.

"I see Israel scattered out there on the mountain
    like sheep that have strayed from their shepherd.
And the Lord is proclaiming, 'They've no one to lead them.
    Let each one go home then and struggle alone there.'"

Micaiah went on to explain how God's angels
      conspired with God to seduce muddled Ahab,
and bring him to justice in this senseless scrape.
      So God, bottom line was behind Ahab's rape.

With that Zedekiah poked him in the nose.
      and challenged the bloodied Micaiah:
"So, you think that you now speak God's holy word?
      Bind him in chains, his word is absurd.

"I'll deal with him when I'm back from the front,"
      and turned to take up his command.
The prophet then teased him, "Nice day on the sod.
      if you *ever* get back, I'm no prophet of God!"

TRACKING WEALTH

T'was a great year for farming in Iowa,
        the rains arrived just as I scheduled.
No blizzards were burying and no late hail tearing
        my current crops cruelly to shreds.

The corn got so high like it might reach the sky;
        the alfalfa in windrows is ready for bailing.
The gold wheat and barley wave in the breeze
        like waves of calm water on quiet, gentle seas.

Now tune up the combines and hone all the sickles,
        the harvest is ready, we'll bring in the sheaves.
With produce like this, I'll retire in my fifties.
        No need to slave on, I can coast through my sixties.

I've made the top bid on a condo near Tampa
        and scheduled a cruise off the coast of Alaska.
I'll see the cathedrals of England and France,
        hear the great music of Handel and Bach.

I'll visit the Nile and the pyramids of Egypt
        and study the sources of Asian phrenology.
I'll surf off Hawaii and ski in the Alps;
        then take a short course on Mayan mythology.

Yet, there is just this one little question:
        Where can I store this incredible crop?
The hay loft is laden, the granary full,
        the corn-crib's already jammed up to the top.

There is plenty to fill up the silos this year.
    The smoke house is loaded with bacon and ham.
Jellies and jams fill the shelves in the pantry.
    We've plenty of squash and potatoes on hand.

C. W. S. would sure take a cut
    and the Red Cross would like some for free.
But if I give it away I could come up short;
    then there'll be insufficient left over for me!

But, eureka! I've got it, here is a solution:
    I'll tear my barns down and build others higher.
I'll have ample room for my entire crop
    and then I'll be free to go on and retire.

Call in the builders, there's no time to waste,
    hire an architect, I'll gather the specs.
He ran to and fro, and hither he darted.
    Here is the blue-print, come on let's get started.

(He paused for a moment in personal reflection,
    and said to himself with smug satisfaction,
"Easy my soul. Eat, drink and be merry;
    you have plenty stored up for a well-earned vacation.")

The man was a fool. He should have known better.
    He was visited that night by the Angel of Death.
"Come now with me, you can't take it with you!
    Your heirs get it all but your last mortal breath.

"You've been graciously blessed with all that you needed
    but seldom saw fit to lend others a hand.
May that be a lesson for all greedy misers,
    a life is not rich with an abundance of things."

"It's not all about how much one has gathered.
      It's giving that counts, losing self is what sings.
Still, if what one has is the measure of wealth,
      consider this proposition:

"What we've spent is all gone. It's consumed, it's depleted.
      It was for a time and now it is not.
What we saved locked in storage there to admire
      was only potential and is starting to rot.

"What we stored in our warehouse for now must be guarded,
      a burden today, ready cash it was never.
What we've given away is all that we have
      and that is our treasure for now and forever."

LOVE'S REALITY

What we know as love is both is and then does.
      Love *is* and love *acts* and that's love's reality.
Two marks will be there where true love's an attraction.
      One mark is presence, the other one action.

FORGIVENESS

How can I know I have truly forgiven
      the one who had once injured me?
How can I tell if my pardon's authentic,
      that I'm really not kidding all others and me?

I know that I should forgive and let go
      as I pray that all others free me.
But how to be sure I'm not duping myself
      when I say that I truly for sure forgive thee?

Overlooking, ignoring, or pleading, "please pardon"
      is just not the same as forgiving.
Those dodges add up to a hedge on the truth,
      a duplicitous move to let me keep on living.

But I yearn for convincing assurance
      that my pardon is straight from the heart.
No games, no phony pretensions,
      a clean slate is granted, a total new start.

Still I know what a fool I can be
      playing tricks on my very own conscience.
I can twist and manipulate truth and façade
      and play I'm forgiving like some mortal god.

Thus my quest for a test of reality
      so I know my forgiving is real.
Solid proof that I have forgiven
      in support of repentance I feel.

If I've really forgiven I've also forgotten.
    The offense is no longer a fact.
It is exactly the same as if it never happened!
    Must I truly forget all of that?

This forgiving is no simple matter.
    There is truly a massive cost.
If I "skip it" or smugly "not notice,"
    in memory that sin is not lost.

I am still in charge of its capital value
    and can still call upon it to strike.
So take care that you tread on me lightly,
    this snake still has venom and bite.

My dilemma's more fully compounded;
    my quest has gone nowhere I see.
I'm not sure that I've ever forgiven
    now seeing how dear it can be.

Is forgiving a real possibility at all?
    Can anyone ever forgive and let go?
It must surely require the grace of a saint
    to truly forgive and to know it is so!

The words from the cross are more haunting than ever:
    "Please Father, forgive them," said he.
"They've simply no way of knowing today
    the torturous price I am now bound to pay."

Just as sure as he bore the pain of those nails
    to save and to gain our full trust,
how now in that grace can I dare forgive you
    as from his cross our Lord forgives us?

Luke 10:38-42; John 11

THE SISTERS OF BETHANY

On the front page of *The News,* always
    the two sisters and their kid brother.
Reporters annoy and hound them relentlessly
    for one snip of gossip or other.

Whether they go, whether they stay
    the paparazzi pursue them what may.
Celebrity status was not their idea
    but daylight to dusk they're considered fair prey.

Mary, the eldest has heaps of appeal.
    It's her aura and pious demeanor.
So zealous, so faithful, so downright authentic
    their pressure is simply pathetic.

Talk about reader-support and raw passion.
    Her presence alone is a favorite target.
Or, as Hepburn often is quoted as saying:
    "I don't know what it is, but whatever, I've got it!"

Then Lazarus, the youngest adored baby brother,
    not really a star in their ladies' circle.
His claim to fame came not in his name
    but in his escape in an after-death miracle.

Their family rabbi called Jesus
    made a sick call too tardy to save.
He called to him anyway, "Lazarus come out!"
    And Lazarus walked forth from the grave.

But Martha's the subject of comment today,
    the meeting is here at her flat.
She is deeply immersed in our tribal tradition
    of hosting the strangers who pause at your mat.

As when Gideon laid on an extravagant feast
    for the guests that stopped by his place
and discovered in time he had hosted angels
    on their way to consecrate *him*.

Martha painstakingly laid out a spread
    fit for a king or a queen,
her best table ware, her fine wine decanter
    while Mary was nowhere around to be seen.

Martha was right in expecting her sister
    to step up and lend her a hand.
That too is a part of our family tradition
    in this taboo-bound, tribal home land.

Preachers are fond of pointing to Mary
    as the one whom Jesus saw fit to show off.
It's her spirituality and devotion to rituals,
    while Martha's so busy just washing the dishes.

We all should be "Marys" the homilists admonish,
    tend to our prayers and hone our humility.
Not busy ourselves with mundane routines,
    stay out of the rat-race and all that futility.

They forget to take note that Martha's the host here;
    the meeting's in her little kitchen.
She's stuck with cookin' and fixen' the vittles while
    we watch the ball game and have one more beer.

In the Sweet Gum Tree

Praise God for the entire world's busy "Marthas!"
        We place our lives at your feet.
We're grateful for Marys and even kid brothers
            but Martha's essential if we're going to eat.

IMPROBABLE CONNECTIONS

Why in the world should I love one like you?
    And why should it be that you also love me?
There's no logic in it, just no rationale,
    no reason that that connection should be!

And what do we make of all the particulars?
    Why *that* someone else and *this* unique me?
No one here on earth claims to have ordained it;
    no heavenly being flew in to proclaim it.

Out of thousands and thousands of matches potential,
    of countless free people near-east and far-west,
how is it these two souls have found one another
    and both are so sure they were made for each other?

Yes, each such connection seemed destined to be,
    like angels arranged each with pious devotion.
While chances of either one finding the other?
    Like snagging a dream in the depths of the ocean!

1 Kings 18:20-40

ELIJAH'S CHALLENGE

Quit waffling on which deity you will follow.
    If Baal is your god, pray then don't look to me.
So maybe Yahweh is the one you will honor?
    Well, choose here today which one it will be!
        Silence from all of the people!

I'm the only voice left of all the Lord's prophets.
    Four hundred and fifty seers shout out your fraud.
I challenge those multiple idol soothsayers
    to prove which of us speaks the true Word of God.
        Mild interest provoking the people.

They pick out two bulls so each side will have one
    to burn on the altar in consummate fire
and reduce them to ashes and dust in a blaze.
    The contest is on; results could be dire.
        Bookies are busily booking the betting.

Baal seers run hither and there and about.
    They're seeking dry kindling and brush for their fire.
They carve up their beef into wolf-gnawing hunks
    and set them in place on the fire's wooden chunks.
        Odds favoring Baal about forty to one.

Four hundred and fifty seers chanting and dancing
    all calling on Baal to torch their heaping pyre.
With swords and with lances mid raving and prancing
    they slash their own bodies and bloody the fire.
        Odds favoring Baal are not now getting higher.

A Red-shouldered Hawk

No god there responding, no singing is heard;
  the altar stays cold and the chops go un-broiled.
Except for the frenzied seers' raving and slighted
  the site is unaltered, the fires still unlighted.
    Bettors on Baal's base are not much delighted.

Elijah takes up with rude, insulting taunting,
  "So where is your god then? Taking a nap?
Is he off on a stroll? Playing cards with his buddies,
  Or, maybe out back there just taking a crap?"
    Baal bettors are fudging their antes.

Elijah then turns to prepare for his case.
  He cleans up the altar, puts new sticks in place.
He slaughters his bull, he cuts it in half,
  puts two sides of beef on the new bricks in haste.
    One prophet competing with hundreds!

He digs a big ditch all around that stone altar
  then calls for a goodly supply of cold water.
Dumps gallons and gallons on beef, sticks and altar
  till water spills over and fills the canal.
    People dumbfounded; all betting corralled.

Elijah backs off soaking wet and assured
  and prays that the Lord will not falter.
Then fire explodes and consumes wood and beef
  including the stone of the altar, then also
    for good, laps up that deep ditch full of water.

Reporters show up there to cover this story.
>They claim that Elijah has cheated.
'Twas gasoline they report, that he poured on the altar
>to cause such a wild conflagration.
>>The bookies? Still looking for water!

The reporters have no credibility.
>With tolerance and patience we've heard their account.
We can see what they have contended.
>But we bask in our confidence serene and contented.
>>Gasoline hasn't yet been invented!

REMEMBERING EMPTY

Remember when the gas tank ran empty!
>There we were stranded. Lord what do we do?
>You told the paralytic to take up his bed and walk.

Remember when the icebox and pantry were empty!
>No manna, no quail. Lord what shall we eat?
>You bade them sit down, broke up the bread and fed them all.

Remember when the pitcher and the cup were empty!
>And you Lord, cried from the cross, "I Thirst."
>Yet the woman at the well found living water in you.

Remember when the bank account was empty!
>And the bills just kept coming in? Lord how do we make it?
>You quieted the waves and commanded the wind, "Be still."

Remember when the closet was empty!
>No new outfit for Easter. Lord what are we going to wear?
>The soldiers cast lots for your coat leaving you hanging there.

Remember, Praise God, that the tomb was empty!
>Forget about the gas tank, closet and pantry.
>The Empty Tomb holds New Life for all.

Matthew 6

Therefore do not worry, saying, "What will we eat?" or "What will we drink?" or "what will we wear?" Indeed your heavenly Father knows that you need all these things. But strive first for the kingdom of God and his righteousness, and all these things will be given to you as well.

Mark 3:20-35

PLUNDERING THE STRONG MAN

The house was jammed, the mob was wild; they tried to eat in vain.
His family thought he was insane and tried to hide their shame.
Some scribes came down from Zion to assess the situation.
They polled the crowd, tallied results, gave this evaluation:

They said "He surely is possessed, inspired by the devil.
How else that performance in a playing field that's level?
He's in old Satan's wicked and firm chain-of-command.
That's how he wields such power with a simple wave of hand.

"Where does that put old Satan," he countered with a wink?
"A house split down the middle? It will crumble in a blink.
A building's but a heap of stone, of mortar and of sand
unless the owner is alert, on guard and takes a stand.

"When out to rob a strong man, don't you think that he will fight?
You first must get control of him and bind and rope him tight.
Then you can raid his larder, his warehouse and his treasure
and plunder all his worldly goods and do it at your leisure."

Then his mother and his brothers came and called for him outside.
"This is a family matter," they pleaded with the crowd.
They still thought he was loony and needed rescuing by them.
They couldn't see that he was there proclaiming God's New Realm.

He got their word, he looked around at those who would be free.
"Look here at these. They are my clan, this is my family tree.
Whoever does the will of God is surely kin to me.
It's the love that shines in faces shows us whose they are, you see."

121

THE DECALOGUE

The mountain's all ready to blow off its summit;
        there's lightning, the thunder is ceaselessly rumbling.
The earth shakes and quakes; there's smoke all around
        like Vesuvius exploding and splitting the ground.

But this isn't Italy, it's God's Holy Mountain
        and God is declaring a pact with his people.
A stiff-necked and a rebellious convention,
        an earth-quake is needed to get our attention.

It's a pact that amounts to a one-sided contract
        revealing what God has designed us to be,
a picture of our fundamental humanity
        set opposite our now existential reality.

It's a pattern that shows how we're now meant to be,
        not a road map on how to go west.
A description of God's plan for us as his beings,
        not a crib-sheet for passing some new-fangled test.

The terms are quite simple and gracious enough,
        our ultimate reference: Reality-Itself.
Serving our Lord has been called, "perfect freedom."
        The first rule makes that the key to the rest.

And if we are true to the accord we are offered
        we'll be a proud people totally free.
The second condition laid on us herein
        underlines that and makes it a clear certainty.

If the Lord is our God exclusively
        then no cause, no value or thing can be!
Nothing we craft for its beauty or use.
        No icon of hero or deified tree

shall ever be counted as sacred and holy.
        The Lord is our God and we worship him solely,
sans mountains and trees and monsters in seas,
        transcending all things of creation.

Then there's the third. God's name will be feared,
        no purse of our lips or gasp in our breath
must ever connect with malicious intent
        God's name, compromising respect for the holy!

The mountain could crumble and fill up that valley
        in responding to such a bellicose volley.
God's name is pronounced in reverence and awe
        and seldom, for sure, even audibly at all.

Saying the name is the start-up of prayer
        in tones honorably cool and uncommonly rare,
never in anger, exclamation or jest.
        So fuss if you must but don't swear on a dare!

The fourth holds the Sabbath as holy and sacred;
        it commemorates God's day of rest in Creation.
We get our six days and even six years,
        but everything takes a break on the seventh.

The mountain's still shaking, smoking and breaking.
        A crevasse has now fractured the base of the hill.
The area is posted, "No admittance past here."
        But Moses and Aaron are called to appear.

123

The priests and the people are warned to stay put.
      They are not to break out or come up the hill.
Leave no footprint near it, it's God's Holy mound.
      The mountain itself is prohibited ground.

God presses his pact on his hard-headed people.
      We see we would win if we followed his way.
But we can't shake the sense that creation is ours
      so we wiggle and squirm testing our puny powers.

"Respect one another," is fifth for review.
      "Honor your tribal identity."
All sorts and conditions are ours to esteem
      but parents are basic in that family tree!

Take pride in the person you're born to be.
      There is no one just like you that you'll ever see.
The same claim is present for all of the others
      so all of them out there are sisters and brothers.

Six, eight and nine we'll take as just one;
      we dare not intrude on another one's run.
Keep our sticky fingers from wondering and roaming,
      respecting what's theirs without any groaning;

possessions and lives and even their name,
      all that they have, and their claim to fame.
Health and well-being included here too;
      respect them as you would have them honor you.

Now back to the seventh, we skipped up above;
      it parallels the second recounted.
As we never revere anything in relations,
      we never use persons as items.

In the Sweet Gum Tree

People are subjects just like you and me.
    Subjects are valued for who they be
not for some other dude's utility.
    (Subjects and *objects* claim clarity.)

"Things" suggest usage as things are intended.
    Persons are loved (often not comprehended).
Adoring a thing takes us back to idolatry
    while using a person is blatant adultery.

The root of both evils, it's easy to see
    is the big "I" that's centered on the big ego, me.
The tenth is the key to this holy contract,
    a rough mirror image of the first one we looked at.

One makes it clear that there's only one God.
    Ten says that that one then sure can't be me.
The whole of this deal hangs on these twin conditions:
    if we travel this way? That's the way it should be!

Desiring is the one that can get us undone.
    It seems full of promise but is really no fun.
Desiring or coveting puts me in the middle.
    The position is God's, see above number One!

Wanting, desiring, grabbing and taking,
    all me-centered acts primed for our quick unmaking.
What is desired is not our concern here.
    It's *desiring itself* that's our reason for fear.

Yahweh displacement is basic in sinning.
    It's the big "I" in me that's the covenant breaker.
We play like we're gods when we're really God's creatures.
    That's havoc with grace and with his design features.

125

So that gives us ten rounding how we should be
    A Gift of our Lord and Creator for free.
We accept it with thanks and pray God we might be,
    all that he wants for us just naturally.

But beware of the snare that's inherent in there;
    we cannot desire to follow God's say
or even pray God to make us that way.
    For wanting to do or to be is still wanting,

a crass violation of rule number ten.
    To covet compliance is still naked sin.
The "I" in the center is back there again.
    "Trying real hard" can never succeed.

The harder I try the stronger me gets.
    The only way in is for me to die out!
Thus, dying to self is the way to new life and
    the only escape from this sin-sodden strife.

The mountain quits quaking, boulders are still;
    a gentle rain's falling, fog whirls round the hill.
Moses descends through the mist and confusion,
    countenance aflame but it's not an illusion.

He covers his face so the glow doesn't scorch us
    yet there in God's presence his face is on fire.
The Lord has revealed his design for his people.
    Creation's in Sabbath; New Life is now here.

We've witnessed a new revelation this day.
    A covenant now sets forth our redefined roles.
Like Noah before us we'll go tie one on
    then return to seek out the gaps and loopholes.

(BCP) Acts 2:42

BAPTISMAL COVENANT

I believe in the faith of the ancient church as set forth in the articles of the Apostles Creed.

I pledge to continue my life's journey at-one with the apostle's teaching and fellowship, in the breaking of bread and the prayers.

I will persevere in resisting evil, and whenever I fall, will repent and return to the Lord.

I promise to proclaim by word and example the Good News of God in Christ.

I pledge to seek and serve Christ in all persons, loving my neighbor as myself.

I will strive for justice and peace among all people and respect the dignity of every human being.

This is my solemn vow to my community, my neighbors throughout space and time and to God; to whom I pray also: give me the wisdom, strength and will to be faithful in the living of it. Amen

A Red-shouldered Hawk

Dedication: St. John Chrysostom, Golden, CO

GOLDEN

The color of Aspens quaking in autumn
    or nuggets panned out of the creek.
The shade of the ale they brew up the river,
    the name of the ore they mine near the peak.

The tone and the resonant quality of speaking,
    the rich mellow music of rhetorical teaching.
The nuggets are verbal, the rich ore is spoken,
    the mother lode is the genius in preaching.

"Golden" is also the tongue of repute
    of Chrysostom of Constantinople.
He is our heritage and him we commemorate,
    an early Church Father and our Patron Saint.

*Almighty God, you have given us grace at this time with one accord to make
our common supplications to you; and you have promised through your well
beloved on that when two or three are gathered together in his Name you will
be in the midst of them: Fulfill now O Lord, our desires and petitions as may
be best for us; granting us in this world knowledge of your truth, and in the
age to come life everlasting. Amen*
    (BCP)

GENETIC MORALITY

My law is not hid in a dark, remote country
    entirely out of your reach,
buried or lost in a tropical jungle
    beyond where no preacher is summoned to preach,
not out there submerged in a deep ocean trench
    in a sea faraway over some foreign beach.

You don't need marines to subdue and control
    or to conquer some far hostile land.
No need for adventurers to ford lakes and streams
    to flesh-out your nation's audacious dreams.
My law is right here, it is written within you
    already as close as it seems.

I am the Law, the Word rooted in you
    in the DNA of your genetic code,
etched on your brain when I first conceived you.
    I'm within your reach and near to your means.
No need to commission explorers to seek me.
    I am, as it were, as near as your genes.

'Tis my very word engraved on your soul
    and now on this day I give you this choice:
life and prosperity or death and its strife.
    Your freedom is also a part of your being,
another gift that I gave you. So here
    in that freedom come now and choose life!

SACRAMENTAL AUTHORITY

The sheaves are brought in from all over the field
     and threshed out here in the barn.
The grain is milled and the flour is kneaded;
     it's bread we receive from the farm.

The loaves with their tasty brown crust
     look and smell like gifts from above.
"The bread is my Body," he said.
     "And the wine in the bowl is my blood.

 "Where two or three come together
     and it's in my name they are here,
I am here with you, I promise!
     It is all our One Body we share."

The woman comes in from her kitchen,
     the man sets his plane on its side.
Men in the field park their riggings,
     all workers pause and abide.

Now we are gathered together
     like wheat brought in from the field,
formed into His body and into His blood
     our hands are his and he makes it real.

It's so blatantly common and simple
     an observer just might not get it.
Our action is holy and blest;
     the People of God are refreshed.

The bread and the wine are the products
    of the earth and the green twining vine.
But what he said, we certainly count on.
    It's on his life that we have been fed.

Now we are his Life and his Holy Body
    at his Work in this time and place.
It's inconceivable, incredibly mysterious,
    but he blesses it never-the-less.

It's the inward and spiritual dimension
    of the outward and tangible expression,
a sacrament you see!
    And a Sacrament is a Holy Mystery.

That's a proclamation not explanation
    confusing the senses and clouding the lenses,
yet it all comes together as Grace.
    And our side of Grace is called Faith.

With Faith of the Actors and Grace in the Action
    the Sacrament flames into Reality!
But if it's not here all at once and together,
    the mystery is missing, the ritual banality.

With faith of the actors omitted, and grace in the action gone. . .
    if the inward and spiritual are hollow,
authority not living or not very strong. . .
    if the intention is totally missing or maybe it's simply wrong,

then what held us enthralled offers no grace at all,
    as fleeting as shadows fainting a wall?
What of believers accepting that fraud?
    I've no idea; that's up to God.

Transfiguration Sunday - Mark 9:2-9; Matthew 17:1-13

LIGHTING THE WAY

Have you ever met Law-Incarnate
        or encountered a Prophet-in-Essence?
They showed up one day on a mountain,
        on a mountain top, effervescent!

The Law looked strangely like Moses,
        Elijah embodied the Prophet,
there to confer with our Lord, the Convener.
        – Sorry, no time for your query.

Jesus, we noted was whiter than snow,
        so radiantly white that he glistened.
Saints Peter and James and Apostle John too,
        were there as ones duly commissioned;

A cloud rolled in enshrouding the scene,
        all very mysterious and eerie.
Dumbfounded we were, confused and astounded
        as we witnessed that strange apparition.

It was an out-of-this-body experience
        with everyone lost in their mission,
like a flying-saucer convention
        as aliens check out their position.

A voice then was heard from deep in the crowd,
        a message intended for you,
"This is my Son, my beloved One,
        listen to him, I implore you."

In the Sweet Gum Tree

The group lost in shadow, each member translucent
      (can't tell if they're corporally real),
when Peter proposes we tack up some posters
      to mark off the site of the meeting.

Jesus insists we are not free to talk yet
      till after he's raised from the dead.
Frightened and wondering we start downhill pondering,
      Is that for sure what he said?

"Keep it a secret," he told us,
      "The unusual phenomenon you've shared in.
You've been given an inkling of life in my Kingdom,
      a taste of just where you are headed.

"A hint eternal of how it is when, where it is now
      and history as surely intentional.
Where time is unlimited, space doesn't matter
      and being is non-dimensional."

It's trying our patience; eternity's here
      and *never* is too long to wait for.
Confused now and blubbering we continue on muttering,
      how to compute all that sage?

But Jesus assures us he'll see it through with us,
      right on to the end of the age.
So here we are cruising, the trail often bruising,
      the story goes on down the page.

Now back to Elijah: why must he come first, pray?
      As in Advent – to get all things ready!
The Son of Man comes, Elijah gives warning.
      Tis the center of history, take notice!

The Law and the Prophets are blessings before us
    assuring our final salvation.
And now we see really, if not all that clearly,
    by light of the TRANSFIGURATION.

OF PURPOSE AND MEANING

The event can claim purpose if someone has willed it,
    no purpose at all if intention's not in it.
Of mortal will, purpose precedes event
    forming its specs and much of its content.

An event without purpose is labeled a mishap,
    by definition there's no one to blame.
It may seem like good luck or a curse on one's name
    but either way, no credit, no shame!

Meaning comes from the event in reflection.
    There may be no meaning on early inspection.
It's God's gift to us forming that event's mystery,
    redeeming and blessing the whole of its history.

It's all up to us to envision and dream,
    to plot a grand course for our highest purposes.
But it's in God's jurisdiction, this blessing-redeeming,
    and in his good time, reveals action's meaning.

HAPPINESS

Don't walk in the way of the wicked
    or travel the path that all sinners tread.
Don't sit at the feet of the scoffers;
    delight in the law of the Lord God instead.

Ponder my law by day and by night. Then
    like trees that grow tall near the water
your soul will not wither, your life will yield fruit.
    In all that you do, you will prosper.

The wicked are chaff that the wind blows away.
    They can't stand in judgment or stay with the just.
The Lord watches over the trail of the righteous,
    the way of the wicked leads all into dust.

*At your command all things came to be: the vast expanse of interstellar space,
galaxies, suns, the planets in their courses, and this fragile earth, our island
home. By your will they were created and have their being.*
    (BCP)

Matthew 20:1-16

THE LAST IS FIRST

The Gringo boss-man had checked out a corner
    of Larimore Square in the slum.
He was hoping to hire available laborers
    not obviously reeking of rum.

The corner he checked was the usual hang-out
    for migrants in need of some work.
They would gather at seven and hope for the best
    but grab any offer even close to their quest.

The seeker found several who seemed to be fit,
    finding zilch in their papers to mention.
They agreed right away on ten bucks a day
    and sped to the field in need of attention.

By mid-afternoon it seemed fairly clear,
    the work could not be completed by dark.
So back to the square to find at least one
    who might lend them a hand in getting it done!

He found one hombre there and promised fair pay
    for working the rest of the day.
They finished by dark. The pay-master came out
    to settle with all workers there.

Gathered about while the boss-man doled out
    tens to each one as seemed fair.
There arose sharp dissension by hicks short one dimension
    who had worked through the heat of the day.

"You paid that guy ten too, though we saw the day through
    the sweat and the blisters, to boot.
We want more for endurance than just your assurance
    that your intentions were pure to the root."

According to Gringo the treatment was fair,
    he had settled for more than agreed.
"Yes, I paid more than due, so what's that to you?
    It's my cash I'm throwing, my seed I'm sowing!"

This is not a tale of injustice,
    but of grace that's beyond simply fair,
and a Denver street encounter
    of and among folk who were there.

The last shall be first is a rule you can count on,
    of how things really work out.
It's even a promise our Lord has assured us,
    of what life in his Kingdom's about!

Inspired by Deborah

TURTLE CODDLING
How Do You Pet a Turtle?

Petting a puppy is mutually pleasant
    as pettee and pettor never doubt.
A lamb or a kitten will also work nicely,
    they're quick to lean into what it's all about.
Chickens and ducks are not great for petting,
    their feathers too easily are ruffled and
their clucking and quacking not that quickly muffled.
    But this pettin' a turtle? I just keep forgettin'!

A baby's a natural for coddling or cooing,
    for tickling and hugging and such.
But caution is due here, a disclaimer arranging:
    be sure someone else is in charge of the changing!
Don't try it with calves for they'll only suckle,
    their tongues are as coarse as sandpaper.
So, a babe is your best bet for a fondling pet yet,
    how *does* one cuddle or fondle a turtle?

Take up a bunny by gripping his ears
    then cradle him under his bottom.
When petting a horse try stroking his neck
    and scratching the base of his ears.
Take care to not look at him straight in the eye,
    he'll take that as a predator's threat.
Avoid all eye contact, he'll soon settle down
    but none of that works with a turtle.

In petting a person mind whether you're fittin',
        it could seem a smidlin' like coddlin a kitten,
a mutually pleasant procedin' indeed.
        But it could be perceived as a hit under way,
so CAUTION's the message conveyed to a mortal
        if hankie-pankie is part of the game-play.
But that doesn't say how one gets under way
        if one's primary hurdle is coddling a turtle.

How can a turtle know someone is petting her;
        there's nothing to stroke but her shell?
Try patting her hide and her head pulls inside;
        try scratching her ears and you'll see you can't find 'em.
Try stroking her neck? Well, that's part of a sweater
        and there's reason to doubt that a turtle can don one.
Her outerwear doesn't allow for it, yet
        how does one coddle a reptile in armor?

Genesis 3

SIN'S ORIGIN

Was sin discovered or was sin invented?
How did it get here? Drive-in or fly?
Why is it that sin is so well-set within us?
And why so deep and so devilishly sly?

Surely somebody dreamed up or imagined it.
Sin couldn't have simply dropped in from the sky.
Things seem to have somehow become some un-mended!
Was sin discovered or was sin invented?

Did sin overwhelm us instantly-suddenly
like a tsunami's wild flooding the hall?
Or was it more slow-like, deliberate, incremental,
as with a creeper ascending the wall?

Or, perhaps it was simply a revelation,
like a new-land discovered or a new law-of-nature?
Maybe it just happened, not even intended.
Was it accidental, or was sin invented?

Was there a Ford or an Edison tinkering?
Or a Wright brothers in someone's bicycle shop,
with gifted, unbridled imaginings toiling
by light of a candle at night after dark?

Did somebody notice the archer, thereupon missing-the-mark,
harmed no one at all, much less the intended target?
So, what's all the furor and who's ill-contented?
Was sin discovered or was sin invented?

Were you there when it occurred to someone or another
        that things needn't always be peaches and cream?
Nor the land flowing with sweet milk and honey,
        that people don't totally need to be free?

Did someone with vastly superior dreams
        come to see that small wrinkles hid under the covers
or a picture not quite square on the wall
        might easily be accommodated, if

we are not too persnickety or fussy at all?
        Maybe the Rulers got some rules suspended.
Does that mean that sinning's no longer a sin?
        But if sinning's not sinful where'd all the fun go?

With no fun at all, a life has no zest! So,
        a life with no zest is life mostly suspended
but let us get back to our quest:
        was sin discovered or was sin invented?

Perhaps a teen driver was first to observe
        the roadway obstructed by one nasty boulder
will not block the carriage completely.
        We'll just swerve around it by cheating the shoulder.

The rut needn't matter if the wheel can get through it.
        We can hose the mud off it a little bit later.
It'll be nearly as clean as the old man intended. Still
        was sin discovered or was it invented?

If the terrain is not flat, the hill too steep to take,
        if the mountain's too rugged or stony to rake,
no need for a cat to level the pathway,
        we'll add two more horses and patch-up the brake.

In the Sweet Gum Tree

We can make it with imperfect grading
        and stay the course nearly as well!
But, the question continues on still un-impended,
        was sin discovered or was sin invented?

There's a definitive tale in mythology
        of a garden somewhere in Eden,
original home of our original parents
        who arrived there 'ere people were breedin'.

They pre-dated clothing and footwear
        unaware they were totally naked.
Till a Tempter came by and opened their eyes
        and all this before sin was intended!

So the first sin might well have been Wisdom.
        The detail's a little bit hazy, as
the Lord checks into the tale:
        the male tries accusing the female

who blames it all on the serpent.
        The snake hasn't even a pinky,
to point it at somebody else. So, the war rages on,
        woman and reptile contended.

Now? Was sin discovered or was sin invented?
        "Discovery" implies sin was there all along.
It must be a part of our created nature.
        Our guilty emotions don't seem to belong

if sin at first was anticipated.
        And why is it sin is connected with Wisdom?
Are we guilty for just being bright? Regardless,
        was sin discovered or was it invented?

We are narrowing our choices, perhaps, more than intended;
      sin might be invited and invented.
It's the blame part that yet remains unresolved,
      though serpent and woman are still co-involved.

I'll take my stand with the woman in conflict;
      that reptile won't likely take this lady down.
We may be condemned and kicked out of the garden
      but the race still ain't aced and I'm betten' on grace!

Hebrews 11:1-12:3

FAITH
Assurance of Things Hoped for
Conviction of Things Not Seen

Faith is a soul resonating with truth
    not one demanding unqualified proof.
Doubt is Faith's partner assuring the soul
    that not-seeing is not a deception.

Embracing our doubt is what Faith is about,
    the conviction that Hope is real too.
We are not to shrink back; we are people of faith
    not of the lost, but for sure of the saved.

Faith is not rooted in striving to have it;
    it's not an objective to win or achieve.
Earning-deserving is not how it works,
    it's really God's gift we are blessed to receive.

Yet with this assurance: What we can't see now
    is indeed what we're presently seeing.
Worlds came to be when God spoke the Word;
    from nothing at all came all Being.

Through Faith our forbearers sought and received
    the total approval of God.
They witnessed the breathtaking power of faith
    from Able and Cain and their offerings.

Enoch escaped the experience of death,
    came directly into God's presence.
He had, as attested, already pleased God
    (and faith's an essential for that).

145

Noah was warned in advance by the Lord;
      he constructed the ark out of cypress.
Then used it to save all his sons and his daughters;
      all others succumbed to advancing flood waters.

Righteousness-by-faith is what he is known for.
      The world, in a perilous predicament
perished in a flood of Biblical proportions
      while Noah got stoned in the first Rainbow Covenant.

But Abraham is our primary example
      of saints who obey without questioning.
He indeed heard the Word though it seemed without merit,
      counter-productive by most people's reckoning.

He followed the order in spite of good sense,
      the epitome of stupid obedience.
Both he and Sarah were sterile as bricks
      yet Isaac sprang forth from those dried up old sticks.

Isaac was known as the child of the promise;
      from Isaac new nations would bring a new-deal.
But Abraham's faith had first to be tested:
      Is it for truth and truly for real?

"Take Isaac, your son, the one whom you love
      to a hill you will one day call home,
a hill called Moriah in the country of Canaan
      and offer him there on an altar of stone."

So Abraham went forth with Isaac in tow
      bearing the kindling for fire.
Isaac, obediently, meekly complied,
      scared and alarmed by his father's desire.

He lay on the altar bound and in terror.
How can this meet the Lord's vow?
But Faith is assurance of promise unseen,
convictions that we cannot deem.

Isaac was saved by a ram in a thicket,
the offering came off as was planned.
The Lord had provided a lamb of his own.
(The mountain was well named *Moriah!)*

Abraham then sent back to his native land
to find a young wife for son Isaac.
Rebekah was chosen and willing and pure
but snitched a few idols (just to be sure).

She had a son Jacob, also called Israel
and that's when things really got going.
He was indeed the prolific one, according to the Lord's promise.
He fathered twelve sons and that just for starters.

We've lost all track of the others.
Still, it's Faith we attend to, not number of brothers
though twelve is the count (each siring a nation).
See, it's faith that's behind all this tribal inflation.

Then there came Moses, true man of The Law.
God spoke to him out of a bush
and sent him on an impossible mission:
to rescue the brick-making lackeys of Egypt,

to bring them up through the Red Sea murky waters
to a land rich and new and just loaded with promise;
another example of walking in faith.
Moses for sure was no "doubting Thomas."

A Red-shouldered Hawk

So, you see we're surrounded on every side
      by such a rich cloud of witnesses.
Let us set sin aside to run persevering
         the race that is now set before us.

We look to Lord Jesus, pioneer and perfector
      who in grace accepted the cross.
He sits on the right of the heavenly throne,
         mission accomplished. Now everyone's home!

TRUST

Don't tell us that, "We ought to trust him,"
    for trust is no moral imperative.
We trust when we're sure that our data are pure
    on just where the other guy's headed.

They said "Lock the wine in the sacristy cabinet,
    you know that we can't trust the sexton.
He'll help himself to a nip now and then
    and none will be left for the Sabbath."

But the truth of it is we can trust the man.
    His course is most surely unswerving.
With near certain faith we can count on the rogue
    to sample the wine when there's no one observing.

It's stealing of course, but that's not the issue.
    The issue in question is the question of trust.
And the question of trust's not an issue of owning
    but an issue of perfect prophetic performing.

Theft has to do with one's right of possession.
    Trust is a function of foreseeability.
The first is a question of simple morality,
    the second put simply, of perceptibility.

If I should perceive that he just doesn't trust me
    it must be incumbent on me to assure
that his take on me is credible to him.
    Transparency is therefore his challenge to me.

If it were truly a question of simple morality
    "shall" or "shall not" might well be at stake.
But since it's a matter of foreseeing ability
    trust, put quite simply is predictability.

In the Sweet Gum Tree

IN MEMORY: those who have faced sudden, violent or tragic death

THE FINAL WORD

When the lines are down
    and the bridges are out
and there's nothing but chaos
    around and about;
the mail isn't moving,
    the rails aren't ringing,
the water's too high
    and nobody's singing.

It's a time of desperation,
    this message must get through.
The meaning isn't really news
    for you already knew!
Yet, it must be said this one last time
    there'll never be another.
Call it impulse, call it urgent,
    guilt or dread, call it whatever.

In this scary demolition
    I can see I've met my end.
Yet never has a truer note
    been written down or said.
I'm not even all that sure
    this letter can get through.
My frantic, honest, sacred
    and final words, *"I love you."*

MISSION ACCOMPLISHED

He hung on the cross, tending to his affairs,
    reviewing his mental check list.
The list was a long one, to-dos from the Father,
    details of the mission assigned him.
Some were new items picked up on the way,
    like the request of the man dying beside him.

He checked items off, the pain was immense.
    He was barely in charge of his senses.
Mission accomplished, duties completed,
    with this brief report to the Father,
        "It is Finished!"

That's all; he gave up his spirit!
    He did what he had been sent for.
Mission complete; check list now clear
    with this brief report to the Father,
        "It is Finished!"

*Keep watch, dear Lord, with those who work, or watch, or weep this night,
and give your angels charge over those who sleep. Tend the sick, Lord Christ;
give rest to the weary, bless the dying, soothe the suffering, pity the afflicted,
shield the joyous; and all for your love's sake. Amen*

*Guide us waking, O Lord, and guard us sleeping; that awake we may watch
with Christ, and asleep we may rest in peace. Alleluia*
    (BCP)

VISION

Behold all is New,
Heaven and Earth and the City.

The Old has worn-out or run-down;
Existence long since run its course.

>   Reality's New, but the Sea is no more
>   nor the church, synagogue or the temple.
>   All of these things, now passed away
>   No part in this brand New Creation.

No more mourning now,
no tears, no fears.
Death no longer reigns in this realm.
Existence is wrapped into Being Itself
And a loud voice is heard from the throne,

>   "Behold,
>   the dwelling of God is with people,
>   it is done.
>   I am the beginning and the end
>   The Alpha and the Omega.
>   If you thirst, take a draught from the spring
>   of the Water of Life.

>   Thirst is no more in this City."

A Red-shouldered Hawk

A Time to Mourn, a Time to Dance; Ecclesiastes 3

AMEN

There was a time in the field on my trusty steed
      galloping, loping or trotting
through the woods, o'er the meadow, on down the trail,
      with an equestrian partner beside me,
when it seemed to me as rich as it gets,
      my horse and I joyfully abiding!
Till the time came and I gave it all up
      for me there would be no more riding.

But I still had the shop, my wood-working hobby.
      Ripping and joining and boring,
sanding and polishing timbers of hard wood,
      hearing the planer's loud roaring.
Smelling the shavings, feeling the grain,
      achieving a rich polished sheen.
What joy and what pleasure, a well-equipped shop;
      then came the time to give up my machines.

Through all of this the blessings of family,
      sharing in joys out-of-pocket.
In kitchen and yard, library and shop,
      living my life: priest, parent and prophet.
But families don't stay together forever,
      kids in their turn will chart their own courses.
Then her time was up and I had to let go,
      my time to deal with un-plotted forces.

Now and then in my dreams I relive those old scenes,
    blessed pleasures are all there once more,
like doing or being at peace in my sleep,
    no need to resort to just counting more sheep.
And then and again I take up my pen
    to commit dream and vision to sermon or ode.
And then and again I still have this yen
    to create something new even though I am old.

Now, no pony or shop companion or call,
    what's an old preacher still have left to do?
Place it all up there, upon God's altar
    with deep and interminable gratitude:
Thank you Father, it sure has been great.
    I have never, ever been bored.
And now it is time to leave it to you.
    It is finished; please bless it dear Lord.

We thank you for the splendor of the whole creation, for the beauty of this world, for the wonder of life, for the mystery of love. For the blessing of family and friends, for the loving care that surrounds us on every side. We thank you for setting us at tasks which demand our best efforts, and for leading us to accomplishments which satisfy and delight us.
    (BCP)

A Red-shouldered Hawk

A RED-SHOULDERED HAWK

IN THE SWEET GUM TREE

SCRIPTURE IN VERSE

SECOND EDITION – NEW POEMS

ECSTATIC CREATING

Where were you when I created the earth?
Tell me, you seem to be so well informed.
Whose notion broke up that primeval accord
when the water was still and the air still unstirred?

Who determined its size? You sure must know that.
Who drew up its blueprint, computed its specs?
Who drafted the land-mass and sketched in the islands?
Who thought up the poles, conceived of the highlands?

Who stretched out the line that marked off its four corners?
How was its foundation formed up and poured out?
Who set down its cornerstone, squared it in place,
engraved their initials and dates on its face?

While all of the morning stars sang out in joy?
The sun and the moon danced and praised their new toy?
Songs of thanksgiving swelled out through the days
and all of God's angels cried out their grand praise?

THE FIRST SIX DAYS

Incubation
In the beginning with creation all set to get going
    before the Big Bang with the chaos still foaming,
the earth had no shape, sense or substance at all;
    nothing was heard from this vacant, blank ball
not even, in those days, a dinosaur's moaning.
    Why, highways and byways had no need of zoning.
Actually, when you get right down to the gist of it,
    there was nothing at all on this sphere or the mist of it.
        (Pre-Creation: Just thinking, that's all)

Day One
The Spirit of God hovered over this mess
    like a broody old barnyard red hen.
Then the Word of the Lord ventured out from the nest
    and the Word that was heard with some effort was "light."
With darkness, constrained earth could be called bright
    with reds, blues and yellows, for starters so right.
But with manifold shades of the spectrum of hues
    and banners of rainbows stacked up for reviews.
        (Darkness now held in abeyance!)

Day Two
So day was created, snatched out of the dark.
    Since then that same cycle's been going.
God's own valuation (for quality control): "It'ldo. It'ldo.
    It'ldo!" Then back to his schema, day two.
The place was a mess, about time to clean up.
    So next on his list: separation of waters -
those up above from those down below.
    So God set a membrane between them just so.
        (A Dome called the *sky* now our brand new partition.)

159

Day Three

The place still cried out for some ordering plan,
  See, rocks scattered hither and yonder.
All trails choked with muck, nearly impassable;
  more structuring of stuff desired where plausible.
God pooled all the water to keep it in channels,
  shoved all rocks and mud into mountains and canyons.
He got green stuff growing wherever it would
  then smiled to himself and declared it all "Good!"
    (Spare water now held in reserve!)

Day Four

Still, no one could see this amazing delight
  since no one thus far had been gifted with sight.
But creation, regardless, in its own momentum
  was there when the blessing of vision was given.
Still, sight doesn't function in darkness of night
  so God set about the perfecting of light.
The sun, moon and stars he set up in the sky
  to mark days and years as the seasons roll by.
    (Sight, now our newest hi-tech reality.)

Day Five

God, filled with delight in the making he'd done
  and the thought that creating could be that much fun,
so delighted, in fact, that on his coffee-break
  he made JOY itself a blessed, cardinal-state.
But creating was waiting and duty was calling
  and still on his list all plant life was looming.
So God spoke the Word and the earth started blooming,
  forests and ferns, a whole world set for grooming.
    (Flora – now flourishing and also perfuming.)

Day Six
It all looked pretty good but with all of this fun
        it was time to give critters their place in the sun.
So God spoke again to craft monkeys and birds;
        he made reptiles and whales and some stuff quite absurd,
dinosaurs, armadillos and cheetahs so fleet and rhinoceroses
        just to stump Adam in naming the beast!
O yes, and on that same fruitful day he formed us
        out of some of that clay and a measure of dust.
            (Fauna now thriving on land, sea, and air.)

Day Seven
God named this day *Sabbath*: re-collect and connect.
        No mundane, no dull, working-day duties to let.
Back off, catch our breath, quiet down, smell the flowers.
        Recall who we are, the rich gifts that are ours.
We're folk of a covenant with a Lord who respects us,
        who loves and protects us. A Lord who expects us
to act, love and look like we live by those themes,
        to center once more on just what all that means.
            Recollecting, Renewing and Resting.
            (Creation most truly, exceedingly good.)

PURSUING PERFECTION

I set out to make a grand table,
 not just *A* table but *THE* table for you!
My intent was to show in perfection, no less
 precisely what tableness is as brand new.
This table would be the manifestation
 of the notion of ultimate table expression,
the tablest table of all of the tables
 that a table-maker in Tabledom could do.

I would make that grand table of hard-wood
 (accomplished wood worker that I'm known to be).
Black Walnut of course is the hardwood of choice
 of most crafters of eastern fine furniture goods.
It will sand to a smooth luster finish
 and do well with fine finishing oils.
I just happen to have some well-seasoned stock
 in my stash of rare native hardwoods.

I had taken it out from that flooded back plain
 where a rambling stream kept things wet.
Two huge walnut stems crowded by sycamores
 had grown there much taller and yet,
after watching them season by season
 I knew that their time had now come,
had gone out with my Stihl chainsaw,
 and my tractor and chains for that reason.

I returned with eight huge walnut logs.
 The sawmill picked up on the project
and filled up my kiln with rough cut walnut stock.
 Scraps kept us warm that whole winter through.
In due course after years in dehydrating clime
 that walnut crop for the shop is quite prime.

In the Sweet Gum Tree

And I'm ready too, knowing what next to do
in crafting that singular table for you.

I went into the kiln to pick out my lumber.
It must be straight-grained and all center cut,
no knots and no sap-wood, veneers not accepted.
About half of that wood should be five quarter stock
all that for the table top. After planing and joining my
table top stock would end up a full four-quarter inch top.
The balance could be standard four quarter rough-cut,
for the rest of that black walnut table raw stock.

Simplicity's the rule, design clean and cool,
no routed edges for this special table.
The legs would be tapered two by two at the top,
one inch square down below on the floor.
The slant taken out from the inside surfaces of each and every leg
leaving the outside corners of all the four legs
precisely square with that five-quarter top.
The table on whole, would look square as a door.

Length by width on the top precisely proportioned
to each other and to the height of the item.
The size of the legs and their appearance of mass
scrupulously suited to their place and utility.
It must have a feel of unerring stability
without ever hinting unneeded redundancy.
It must be perceptibly utilitarian but
superbly sublime in its own simple beauty.

The rails, side and end, mortised into the legs,
rails slightly recessed on the bottom edge.
With this the table begins to assume
a decidedly southwest appearance – so soon!
A few more decisions as options come up
such as timing that grand presentation

and my table is ready to hand off to you.
　　　　But that tablest of tables was never in view.

I have completed a lovely, black walnut, southwest, oil finished,
　　　　hand-rubbed, utility, living room table for you.
A table we'll both appreciate for year upon year even after it's new.
　　　　Still, just *A* table, not table*NESS* as per plot!
A particular table, an exquisite model of tableness too.
　　　　No one could find fault in such well-fashioned case
of table creating this side of the earth or in heaven above.
　　　　But the ESSENCE of table, this table is not!

It's no pantry table for rolling out pie-dough,
　　　　no butcher's block for cutting up meat.
It is not a footstool for just resting your feet,
　　　　nor a place where eight diners might sit down to eat.
It is no sewing table or a setting for Bridge,
　　　　nor a saddler's worksite for stitching up leather.
This table is useless for most of those uses
　　　　but as example of tableness, just cannot be beat.

Humanity, at first, an IDEA in God's mind;
　　　　the intention envisioned was two of mankind
so no one in the clan need ever feel lonely.
　　　　God's PLAN was mankind in perfection of course,
but, in truth we appeared in specifics and worse.
　　　　The specifics turned out to be myriad in number.
Not just male and female but variants in millions
　　　　as we all settled in to our own lone pavilions.

Alas for all planners' attempts at perfection.
　　　　They're doomed at the start by too many courses.
Dreams and inventions spring forth far too fast
　　　　for our crafting skills to keep pace with the forces.
Try as we must we can't see all the options.
　　　　Not will or desire or sin holds us back
and it's certainly no lack of encouraging voices.
　　　　In creating a thing there are too many damn choices.

IMPROBABLE FORCES AND OBJECTS

It seems fairly certain to me that there just shouldn't ever be
  a thing that can never be moved, or ever be made never free.
And for rational people quite equally implausible
  a force just not virtually, but utterly unstoppable.

One or the other could be, I surmise,
  but taken together the thought's no surprise
that the two won't hold water as ideas defendable,
  even one at a time they don't sound all that credible.

Peaks of the Rockies might look like contenders
  for objects that aren't even remotely removable.
A tsunami off raging across the Pacific
  sure seems as unstoppable as any force ought to be.

But put them together and what do we find?
  A gorgeous Grand Canyon; it just takes some time.
The grandeur of that canyon is evidence enough
  there is no such substance as bland, boring, fixed stuff.

It also shows clearly through twisting and churning
  all forces are subject to routing and turning.
Such powerful might and resilient material
  lifts creative potential to highest performing.

It seems an example of God's creativity
  for parents and teachers of his inspired people.
What looks like unmalleable or maybe unstoppable
  is Creation evolving while not very audible.

ADAM and EVE

As God finished up his great burst of creation
        and things here on earth far exceed expectation
there's still this one question demanding attention:
        just how to awaken this grand new invention?

God's yen was for friendship from within that scheme,
        its own innate love of great wonders now seen.
A caring and sharing companionship holy
        for clearly the Lord prefers not being lonely.

God fashioned a man out of clay and of dust,
        pumped into his lungs vital life-bearing stuff.
He planted a garden in Eden's east end,
        homestead and estate for the first tribe of men,

a ranch and a spread for this new entrepreneur
        but the creature seemed lost in his new paradise.
The Lord could see something was sadly amiss.
        The man, like his God, had a yen for a friend.

To concoct a companion for his lonely "Adam"
        was first on the list for his next creativity.
God made birds and fish, things that crawl on the ground,
        elephants and cats, even raccoons and hounds.

He brought them to Adam for naming and listing.
        Whatever he called them, that was its name.
Then he made Eve with her long wavy hair,
        set her in their midst with no special fanfare.

Man, stunned and dumbfounded, eyes now opened wide,
　　ogled in awe at the splendor at side.
Delighted, excited, stunned with what God did!
　　And how he could do that, and all with one rib?

She was gorgeous, voluptuous, a superb work of art.
　　He was excited, delighted, so eager to start,
yet awed and too frightened to know what to do.
　　Still, all things considered, now his turn to move.

Yet he stood stunned and dumbed, stiff and frozen in place,
　　a little stand-off-ish, some red in the face.
She too, hesitating but sure in responding
　　to his lame excuses for groping and fondling.

With nothing in mind but a new population,
　　they quickly went into their grand copulation.
They did get it off, of that never fear.
　　How else to explain how we came to be here?

OUR GLORIOUS GOD

Hooray to our God! Alleluia, hooray!
    Credit the Lord with all glory and power.
Recognize his great strength, his magnificent fame.
    Worship and hallow his glorious name.

His voice thunders over the furious waters.
    He subdues raging seas; he quiets the tempest.
His splendor outshines all the glory of kings,
    his voice like a heavenly choir now sings.

Credit the Lord you tin gods and dumb idols.
    Credit the Lord with all glory and strength.
Credit the Lord the praise due our God's name.
    Worship him now and forever the same.

The speech of the Lord is charged up with power.
    His thunderbolt mangles the tall cedar forests.
He smashes the redwoods of Lebanon's moats;
    all the trees dance around like little kid goats.

Mountains and deserts tremble in terror.
    His lightning strikes fear everywhere.
Live oak trees are stripped of their foliage and branches.
    Ravaged are forests and wasted are ranches.

All people cry out to the Lord, Alleluia!
    Our Lord reigns in glory forevermore.
He has rescued his people; he makes them all strong.
    In grace and in peace we are blessed all day long.

STEWARDSHIP PRIORITIES
Cathedrals and Heifers

My support of my church is not charity;
    it is a cost-of-living necessity.
As with shelter, utilities, some meat on the table,
    and clothing to cover my back as I'm able.

These are, as they say, the *essentials*,
    as distinct from *discretionary expenses*
among which I'll make my selections
    of items I care for but don't count essentials.

Such as feeding the hungry folk all around
    or building a cathedral right here on home ground.
Those worthy causes and needs do abound
    with justified claims on resources available.

Doctors sans Borders, an obvious selection
    supporting professional medics online.
The Heifer Project, also a good choice, such
    creative disbursing of offerings of mine!

The Salvation Army, all-time steadfast pard
    in the funding of projects right here and abroad.
And the *Relief and Development Programs*
    of all of our main-line communions.

And with all of that we are just tagging starters
    in finding reliable servanthood partners.
At first it would seem to be a no brainer
    if food or first-aid is the need of my neighbor.

A Red-shouldered Hawk

Then my call's to be there as soon as I'm able,
            to help with whatever resource is available.
Yet there is this one mystery still left to resolve
            since earliest times, the very beginning,

Yes, even before the beginning of sinning
            our kind has never made that our clear choice!
When culture itself had hardly got going
            in those booming days of history's first glowing,

even then mankind's yen was for Beauty and Sweet,
            even then when our stomachs were yearning for meat
our hearts still cried out for a Cathedral Seat.
            Simple caring for self could always be beat.

Since earliest, dim, dawning of mankind's beginnings
            the needs of the soul and those of the body
have made co-demands on the craft-art of hands
            since earliest, dim, dawning of folk in these lands!

Conscience is with us, has helped form our living
            and so all of our choices incur risk of sinning.
We must make decisions, there's no other way.
            But decisions imply risk of ruing the day.

Since earliest times in America or Egypt
            cathedrals and temples, pyramids and forts
have garnered mass assets and public assent.
            Essentials and *Beauty* have both found supports.

If we were inclined to simply make poverty
            our exclusive, our first and primary priority,
the world would accordingly have no glorious art,
            no grand marble carvings, no fabulous paintings

and no great cathedrals in anyone's homeland,
    the nations completely impoverished,
all beauty de-facto abolished,
    and the poor would still be here among us.

So here is what I will do: I'll tithe my discretionary budget
    and commit that small portion to Beauty and Love.
The balance of those discretionary amounts
    I'll contribute to causes like those up above.

If, after all of those funds are exhausted,
    I still feel the yen to contribute again.
then I'll have to find some way to check their credentials
    and agree that Cathedrals indeed are essentials.

CENTERING DOWN

Rejoice in the Lord every day – all the day.
I mean, revel in God without ceasing.
Help others to know that you have their back.
The master is coming, their master and mine;
he could be arriving here now any time.

Don't get all beleaguered, don't worry or fret.
Let prayer be your knee-jerk response.
In short order you'll notice his comfort and grace
fill you with harmony, quiet you down
with him in the center, your feet on the ground.

Think about all that is noble and true,
commendable, pleasing and just. Whatever is pure
or worthy of praise, pleasing or basically good.
Think about these and your life will be whole,
you will then have Christ's peace in your soul.

THE LITTLEST ANGELS

Two juvenile angels now had their new wings
    and permits to travel through all times and things.
A bit inexperienced yet eager to go,
    both halos still wobbly but tied down just so.

Called Ralphie and Ailee the two went on duty
    at midnight, First Advent, that year in November.
Their first mission order, not long in arriving
    had both them deployed to some shepherds abiding.

A lonely green slope with their flock gently lowing,
    the shepherds of course had a small fire going.
About this same time two youths were seen hiking
    along old game trails that some used for biking.

The kids seemed unsure of the way they should travel
    when they saw the sheepherder's camp on the knoll.
It was late in the day, about time to bed down.
    The sheepherder's camp was the best bet around.

They walked to the camp and just hoped for the best.
    With a little good luck they might get a night's rest.
The youngsters out traveling that bright winter night
    were Joseph and Mary on their destined flight.

The City of David was their destination.
    Travel was tough for one now great with child.
But courage is grace for one facing the wild
    and grace was that night with this young woman mild.

173

So Joseph and Mary put up that cold night
      in a sheepherder's camp under stars shining bright.
The shepherds were quick to share campfire and vittles
      with two lonely youths on some strange, holy flight.

Thus, two frightened kids found safe haven that night,
      completely exhausted from their harried flight
and both were soon sleeping, escaping their fright
      while shepherds kept watch under star-light so bright.

Near half past that midnight God's two smallest cherubs
      by chance came upon sleeping shepherds and their guests.
They felt wondrous joy at their chance to show spirit,
      about to explode but not very coherent.

Ralphie stepped up to take charge of their sing.
      Out poured "Hallelujah," and "Glory we bring!"
But Ailee's harp strings were hung up in her wings
      and the sounds that came forth were but screeches and dings,

a disjointed tangle of harp string and feather!
      While feathers of wings should remain matched together
and wings in their own right enfold well retracted,
      still, musical numbers must be well enacted.

This mangling of harp strings and ruffled-up feathers,
      discordant abounding of echoes resounding,
angels confused and untrained in their singing,
      two youths now awake with ears sorely ringing.

The kids now alert sat there rubbing their eyes,
      not able to fathom this midnight surprise.
Then Mary now stretching, reached for her kimono
      while carefully studying two cherubs' portfolio.

"I think that I got it. A welcome committee's
        come out here tonight to greet our new King."
But she had to keep smiling at antics and things
        of these two littlest angels not used to their wings.

Then Ralphie, the bold one committed to mission
        backed off and burst forth, a high-tenor musician:
"Behold, hear good tidings of glad, happy show.
        Aah Ailee, How is it that line's 'sposed to go?"

Mary now laughing, hand over her face,
        tossed back her black tresses and joined in the pace.
Through all this the shepherds slept on undisturbed.
        "I see what you are up to," she cried unperturbed,

"To tell the whole world that their new king is near.
        But you're off on your timing, that day is not here.
The heavenly chorus is not serenading,
        the shepherds are not gussied up for parading.

"The stars are not yet aligned as predicted.
        And this is the point that is truly the key:
My time, the great Kairos, is not yet fulfilled!"
        So Ralphie and Ailee retreated, both stilled.

But Joseph was quick to assure them at once
        this was just a rehearsal and all was not lost.
So at the true Kairos we *will* all be ready,
        ready to welcome new life and its realm.

Then all the world cheering from Paris to London,
        Pretoria and Moscow, New York and Saigon,
singing their praises and glad hallelujahs,
        a new day is breaking! Come welcome the dawn!

175

Ailee checked her wrist watch. "Hey, Ralphie, she's got it!
    It's just half past Advent; we're jumping the gun.
We still have some time yet to get all things ready.
    So two littelest angels backed off calm and steady.

Later that week red lights flashed in their faces.
    All parties were called to their pre-assigned places.
The shepherds had staked out new range for their sheep.
    The stars were aligned now in heaven so deep.

The animals quietly chewing their cud so,
    while Joseph found Mary a cozy, clean bedroll.
Just then the whole night sky seemed like to explode
    with trumpets and trombones and some seraph's harpsichord.

When all of God's angels burst forth in a chorus
    and there right along just in front of the florist
sang Ralphie and Ailee in now perfect harmony,
    halos a'glistening as all halos ought to be.

That whole night's performance was given top tribute
    by a Confessions Committee of those who contribute.
And special acclaim went to two of their actors
    with foresight to trigger that full-dress-up practice.

So this night, again we recall and are blessed
    by these cosmic events we will ever confess.
Our Savior comes to us as God's Word Incarnate,
    in God's holy time and his time can't be late.

Yet, two fumbling, young, heavenly overachievers
    of God's High Command of Good News Believers
near busted up history's most Central event
    by jump-starting Christmas in middle-Advent.

1 Samuel 3:1-10

THE CALL OF SAMUEL

Eli was young Samuel's first pastor and priest.
    Hearing God's Word was quite rare on his beat.
Apparitions, not really widespread or revered;
    discouraging times for Eli, man of God.

Samuel, a lad, did not yet know the Lord.
    In the darkness of night a voice called out his name,
"Samuel!" "Samuel!" He heard it quite clearly.
    "Here I am," answered he, as he hastened to Eli.

Eli, nearly blind, tried to comfort the lad.
    Perhaps it was only a dream had disturbed him.
In the darkness he gave him a comforting hug,
    then caringly sent him to his sleeping rug.

Now, Samuel did not get to sleep right away
    when the Lord called out to him yet once again.
Again Samuel thought 'twas Eli was the caller
    and again Eli claimed that it was not his holler.

On the third call that night Eli sort of caught on,
    realizing the caller was surely the Lord.
So while comforting the lad he explained this new view.
    "Tis the voice of the Lord that is calling to you."

So his counsel this time could be synchronized
    with Eli's new sense of conditions.
He explained all of this to a sensitive boy
    and told him precisely how he should respond.

Samuel returned to his cold sleeping pad,
    quite sure by now that the Lord was his caller.
When the voice came again the boy sat at attention.
    "Speak Lord, your servant is listening."

PRIMARY ACCOUNTABILITY

So, they don't want to eat pork?
    They shouldn't be made to eat pork!
Who are we to insist
    that they should enjoy roast pork?

So, they say that the Sabbath is holy?
    Saturday is their day of rest?
Who then are we to tell them,
    that Sunday observance is best?

Some folk just see things a little bit differently;
    no need then for us we should expect unanimity.
Who are we to be judge over their contradictions?
    Let all be affirmed in their own clear convictions.

The Lord is our common Father as he watches over us all.
    The choices we make we don't make in a vacuum.
They are made in full deference to him.
    So, are we to be judge or a jury?
    We are far and away too dim!

We eat in honor of God, and we fast in our Lord's holy name.
    So whether we eat or in discipline refrain,
we do so in honor of God. For he is both Lord of the free
    and Lord of those bound by a vow to abstain.

If we are to live, we live in the Lord.
    Or if we're to die we die in his name.
So no matter, live on or die now we still are the Lord's.
    Christ is our Lord in whatever domain.

For to this end Christ lived and to this end he died,
        to be God of the living and Lord of the dead.
We are not to be judge of our sister or brother,
        just to remember what someone has said:

"As I live, every knee shall bow down to me,
        every tongue shall give praises to God."
So, that's where we are, just take it from me.
        We are accountable to God, and so it shall be.

A CLEAN SLATE

There are new days approaching, new life to be found.
    No kidding, no horseplay, no messing around.
A new covenant unrivaled where everyone wins,
    new conventions, conditions – now let that sink in!

Not just a rehash of that old tired pact
    I made with your forefathers many years back,
when I freed you from slavery and degrading labor
    and gave you a new chance to be a good neighbor.

An agreement you all disregarded and scorned
    without even thinking, though hadn't I warned?
Yet for me it was sworn to, a sacred accord;
    it was treasured by angels, revered and adored.

My new law will not be a handout on paper,
    scribbled on clay or say, etched with a scraper,
but carved in your heart, engraved on your brain
    will the letter and spirit of my law remain.

Make no mistake I will still be your God.
    There is no room at all you should doubt about that.
And you'll be my people; it's already your leaning,
    but no special teaching and no voter screening!

For all of my people will then know the truth,
    the most innocent child to the wisest of prophet.
Sins not just unnoticed, but totally forgotten,
    guilt not just passed over – entirely absolved.

Romans 7:7ff

DESIRE'S RELENTLESS PROGRESSION
"I" from Temptation to Guilt

From temptation to guilt a boundary's in place
    with numerous checkpoints to pause or save face.
The name of that force-pushing will is desire.
    Temptation's the start of that treacherous race.

Those checkpoints that mark from temptation then on,
    begin with an *itch* or an *urge*, nothing wrong.
With *wish* the long reach is beginning its stretch.
    Seek shows curiosity's now onto the stretch.

As seek grows to *want,* desire's now stirring,
    then to a *need* where desire's emerging.
Need ups the ante with reason or purpose.
    Requirement confirms that the purpose is growing.

Crave is desire's unquenchable appetite.
    With *covet* bald jealousy enters the fight.
Lust is desire on fire with mad passion.
    Demand is desire ablaze and in sight.

Compulsion's desire plum out of control.
    And *Guilt* is desire's grand victory festivity.
It's "I" that's near middle in every desire;
    "I's" now on dead center in guilt.

EPIPHANY FANTASY

They entered the house and saw the child in the arms
of Mary, his mother. Overcome, they kneeled and
worshipped him. Then they opened their luggage
and presented gifts: gold, frankincense, myrrh.
                              Matthew 2:11

It was the strange, bright night sky that first got our attention,
   not northern lights, satellites or some odd constellation.
Nor just a falling star streaking through night, but a single star
   calling, persistently beaconing, calling, calling . . . a' calling.

A North American phenomenon as far as we could tell,
   no way of really knowing just how wide that night oddity fell.
From Jimmy Salmon fishing on the Kotzebue cold north sound
   to Rodrigues de Hernandez on a high Mexican jungle mound.

A Canadian Mountie in Kamloops,
   a home-maker of western Penn;
they too had seen the strange night sky,
   they too had experienced the yen.

A compelling message was falling,
   like someone was out there and calling,
a sentinel way up there a'calling;
   repeatedly . . . beaconing . . .calling.

We gathered together in Denver,
   from all corners of our fair homeland.
But how to respond to a signal
   that seemed to just sparkle and stand?

In the Sweet Gum Tree

A Navajo maid from Four Corners
  had also joined up with our band.
It was clear she would be our fair princess,
  representing our common homeland.

So we decked her all out in beaded buckskin
  with an eagle feathered crown.
Set her up on a painted pony
  on a blanket of woolen and down.

By then we had all figured out,
  she was blessed with rich spiritual power.
And she was the one who could lead us
  to wherever the star was a'calling.

All the time the star stayed there compelling,
  quiet but seemingly, steadily yelling.
The princess in sync with the star's subtle signals
  guided us all in our common replying.

In a chariot of feathers and valiant endeavors
  and audacious deeds never falling,
we traversed all space-time in our fateful response
  to a star ever calling us—calling and calling.

The star is still out there a'calling,
  persistently calling and calling,
and now with a princess to guide us,
  a princess with us all on our calling.

Yet now a new question to haunt us:
  callers are bearers of presents.
Tradition demands it, visitors bear witness;
  gifts are a part of all visitor calling.

The Northern lights from Alaska,
  a magnificent falls from the lakes,
a Redwood Pine and a Douglas Fir
  from out on the western brake.

Succotash and new spuds from back on the farm,
  apple pie a la mode for dessert.
And now we were set to pay our respects
  to wherever the mystery star takes us.

A princess astride a painted mount,
  so eager to lead in pursuit of the dream;
a lad from the north and a kid from the south
  and two others from somewhere between.

In a chariot of cotton and anthracite
  we traversed at least two of the poles,
arriving at last at a battered old shed
  with a manger and makeshift bedroll.

And there lay the babe on a bed of sweet hay
  at over six pounds boasted angels.
Wrapped up in a sheet, at peace in his sleep,
  his Father's good will all around us.

He was dreaming of fairies in forests just then,
  with mushrooms for little white stools.
One stood in a nook reading from a big book,
  the others responded, "Amen."

We presented our American passports
  as a legitimate claim to our right.
But the guard at the shed didn't stamp them right then;
  security was terribly tight.

All the time that bright star, stayed over the barn
  broadcasting the Presence within.
Our gifts were received with joy and delight
  by the angel on duty just then.

The barn was jammed full of seers and kings
  offering their gifts of good will and fine things,
arriving from out beyond Venus and Mars,
  some others from some of the far-away stars.

They traveled by stage coach, steamship and rail
  and one chap arrived by first class air mail.
Their travel was clear by rigs parked in the rear,
  a carriage of gold, a posh Pullman car,

Air Force Number One, and then, just for fun,
  a catamaran and a little kid's trike,
a sleigh and a shay, a buckboard and a boat,
  and a shiny new two-wheeled Schwinn bike.

Those folk had come in, by summons they said,
  by a star that hung over them calling.
Don't take my word for it. I only report
  how they all explained their responding.

We had paid our respects. It was time to depart.
  With our princess we called up her pony.
We took a shortcut skipping Nome and Stockholm,
  then taxied down Old Milky Way.

Started descent o'er a Grand Teton tent,
  commandeered mighty Mo. for our glide path;
followed Erie Canal, circled Chesapeake Bay
  and landed back home in the U. S. of A.

GRATEFUL INDEBTEDNESS

You own the heavens; the earth is yours too.
    You created the whole cosmic she-bang.
You laid the foundations of all that's about.
    You told north and south just where to hang out.

The rivers and mountains delight in your name,
    mighty your arm and the power of your grip.
Your footing is righteousness, justice your throne.
    Your face is on fire, truth and love are your own.

Delighted are we to know your festal shout
    as we dance in the light of your Presence.
We daily rejoice in your righteousness Lord,
    and jubilantly sing your name as adored.

Your own vibrant beauty now glows on inside us.
    Your graciousness has us all walking on air.
For all that we are or about which we sing
    we are in your debt, O our Lord God and King.

Psalm 103:1-13

HYMN OF PRAISE

All that is in me sing praise to the Lord;
    all that is in me bless God's holy name.
Do not fail to notice his benedictions.
    Praise him forever and ever the same.

He forgives all our sins, heals all our diseases,
    redeems us from hell with his mercy and love.
He calms all our fears with goods we desire;
    we soar like an eagle and coo like a dove.

With justice to all the oppressed, all the victims,
    revealing to Moses and Israel's children.
With mercy and grace and not easily angered,
    sans endless nit-picking and unending scolding.

We haven't been treated as we deserve,
    or condemned for our gross sinful dealings.
His love is so strong for we who adore him,
    a heaven's iron dome for our ceiling.

Far as the horizon, sunrise to sunset
    are our sins kept distant from us.
Like a doting parental love for the child
    is our Father's fondness toward all of us.

ENTANGLEMENTS

The most vexing challenge in giving a gift
        is for sure in just letting it go.
Most tempting of all in turning it loose
        is the urge for a peek, as you know.
The fate of whatever the gift that was given
        should be no concern of mine.
Yet the urge to check out its enduring impact
        grabs onto me every last time.

This enigma reveals my persistent failure
        in the genuine giving of me.
When dangling strings still cling to the thing
        my offering for sure was not free.
To assure the gift's free as all gifts claim to be,
        I must certainly neutralized be.
With me nullified and grace recognized,
        a gift is a gift then you'll see.

It's a challenge to me then to set me aside
        if a straight forward gift I'm to offer.
But how claim the task when I am the block
        to all that goes into the coffer?
A conundrum in logic now there in my head;
        how could I have gotten so dense?
I'm damned if I do and damned if I don't
        and in hell while I sit on the fence.

If I give the gift then it's I must let go
        or the gift is entangled with me.
But if I give the gift it is tied to me
        regardless of what I decree.

In the Sweet Gum Tree

The only way out if the gift's to be free
    and I be the genuine giver
  is the gift and the giver be joined into one
    with no clear distinction whatever!

By deduction I see that the only real gift
    that in truth I can offer to you,
  is my life and my will since anything else
    by entanglement adds those two, too.
A gift is not taken so lightly; lives are paired, bared
    and dared and not spared at all.
  It's serious business, this giving of gifts
    and could presumably end in a fall.

Now let's see if I got all this wisdom down rightly
    in grasping just what I can do.
  When moved to give gifts there is only one gift
    that in truth I can offer to you
and that is myself, my very own self,
    and I'm the lone one who can do it.
  It's the ultimate gift, naught can compare
    and furthermore none can undo it.

It appears there is no letting go of the gift,
    it's a kind of whole-hearted demand.
  The gift that I offer is my total being;
    now I see nothing else I command.
No trade, charm, token or trinket
    and certainly no trite "gift exchange."
  It's me, nothing less, nothing more;
    it's me no one else can arrange.

I wonder if thoughts such as these crossed His mind
    as he contemplated his end.
  All in a day's work for those holding him down
    while jamming the thorns on his head.

189

He blessed them right there while bearing the pain
    that they were inflicting on him,
  and as he still thirsted had mercy and grace
    to redeem the one nailed up beside him.

The deepest entanglement ever conceived of
    in God's all-inclusive creation
  involved string and rope and ribbon and chain
    in tangles at every last station.
Rough wood and hard nails we'll add to the lot
    assuring well-snaggled entangling.
Fold in and layer with love, peace and grace
    assuring no tag's left a'dangling.

Awesome, mysterious, outrageous and bold,
    our Lord in committing his life.
But our fate as well was determined that day,
    our humanity hung in that strife.
In this act the gift and the giver are one.
    Paul calls it a whole "New Creation,"
and swears we're there too, wrapped into that gift
    and part of that humiliation.

There's many a hero might save some poor slob
    by risking of life and of might.
And even rare cases of lives sacrificed to save stupid fools
    from their well-earned plight.
But His offering in the fullness of time was in spite
    of our steady resistance
  into Ultimate Being beyond space and time
    to a realm that transcends all existence.

It's the gift of all gifts and endures as the model
    of how mortal giving should go.
We offer ourselves in final commitment
    skipping objections and frivolous show.

He challenged old Satan in his own domain,
    as he marched victoriously through it.
Then gave up his life in sublime human giving,
    for only as God could he do it.

Psalm 23

MY SHEPHERD

The Lord is my guardian shepherd;
    he understands all of my needs.

He guides me to fresh, verdant pastures
    and leads me to clean sparkling springs.
He inspires my soul and my wondering dreams,
    he shows me a safe way to home.

Though my journey will take me
    through treacherous terrain
fear will not o'ertake me, nor his staff forsake me.
    His protection is present at my every turn.

Right here in the midst
    of these foreboding surroundings
I'm blessed with his gifts in abundance.
    My cup's overflowing; the feast is sublime.

His goodness and mercy are with me through time
    and I'm safe in his mansion forever.

PAUL'S CONFESSION

So you love to boast of your high-class credentials;
    well consider mine too, taking note of essentials.
I was born one of God's chosen people, for starters,
    circumcised the eighth day of my circumscribed life.

I was raised up and trained as a strict Pharisee
    with degrees and top honors in all aspects of law,
blameless in keeping traditional minutiae,
    the most zealous rival the church ever saw.

Yet now I regard all these credits as losses,
    for now I have come to a knowledge of Christ.
Believe me, it's perfectly clear to me now
    that all I once stood for is now sacrificed.

Now that I know him and his saving grace,
    those old merit badges once bragged of and treasured
are not worth the ribbons that once served to name them
    nor even the breath I now use to defame them.

So bottom line, I have nothing to boast of,
    no righteousness of my making or merit.
No credits earned from avoiding of flaws,
    no praises, no honors for minding of laws.

But I do boast of righteousness straight from our God;
    righteousness based on my faith in our Lord.
For I do know the Christ and the power of him risen.
    I know of his death and now share in him living.

I don't mean to say I've already achieved these
and I don't mean to claim any fine expertise.
But such is my goal and such drives me onward;
for this I've been called and in this I'm now pleased.

So I forget all that history and tribal tradition.
I see what's ahead and there's nothing I lack.
I press toward the goal; I'm off and I'm running.
Just watch me make track for I'm not turning back.

SISTERS

Mothers have sisters and fathers have sisters;
all of those sisters are aunties to me.
Grannies have sisters and grandpas have sisters;
they are my grand (older)aunties you see.

Brothers have sisters and cousins have sisters.
Neighbors and playmates can have sisters too.
Colleagues have sisters and bosses have sisters.
Prisoners and captives have sisters, a few.

It may be near half of the world's precious people
are kin folk that we know as sisters.
But the finest, most treasured sweet sisters there be
are sisters of sisters, just like you and me.

A Red-shouldered Hawk

Mark 13:24-37

ON ALERT

The sun will have totally shut down by that time;
      the moon will not rise to provide its soft light.
The stars will have fallen from out of the sky
      and all cosmic powers will be trembling in fright.

Just then will the Son of Man be revealed,
      enthroned in grand clouds of power and might.
His angels will be there, out searching the four winds,
      gathering the chosen from left and far right.

From the fig tree learn this simple lesson:
      when the branches are green and sprouting new vines
you know that the summer is right near at hand.
      Any dummy can see the plain truth of those signs.

So, these too should be seen to be obvious truths
      when you see all these signs I've just mentioned.
That he has arrived at your personal gate
      and this will take place in your own generation.

Of heaven and earth you will not be aware,
      but through all this turmoil my word will be there.
The precise hour or day, no one will know when
      excepting the Father above us, in heav'n.

So, beware, stay awake, keep alert and no napping.
      He could come at cockcrow or evening or dawn.
How could you discern it; where is your alarm?
      He could catch you sleeping; your cause would be gone.

So, I'm telling you now like I tell all the rest:
      stay alert! Keep abreast of the signs.
Take no rest, on your toes, it's no time for sleep.
      Whadya think yet? You're off countin' sheep?

Mark 15-16:8

LITTLEST ANGELS - EASTER

The women had watched from a distance, you see
     having followed and served him throughout Galilee.
Now deep in despair and pulling their hair
     they continue their watch as he strangles up there.

He was sentenced to die on the cross this last Friday.
     The men had run off, scared out of their wits.
The gals will not likely be noticed, of course
     as they go about womanly care of the corpse.

They had gathered their oil and paraphernalia;
     by dawn they had everything ready to go.
The interment, not rightly attended before,
     now with Sabbath behind they will finish the chore.

God's two littlest angels here also today
     as they'd ministered to him in his wilderness fear
while his mission on earth was becoming more clear.
     So again they're on duty as he wraps things up here.

The angels weren't there to work out his escape,
     nor to block or divert any worldly momentum.
They know as does he, he will see this thing through.
     Timing is critical. They had learned that truth too.

Their task is ministry, to be with him in prayer.
     Not tamper with history unfolding in there,
to support and redeem not obstruct or be seen,
     two little cherubs like phantom marines.

So, Ralphie and Ailie, (the stone now removed)
     take up their posts in the now empty tomb.

195

It's nearly daybreak and the sky is ablaze
      with red and orange streaks of morning's soft haze.

The women creep warily nearer the crypt
     when they see that the stone appears to have slipped.
They stoop and peer into the tomb's chilling darkness.
      Their eyes soon adjust to the light's eerie absence.

So, cautiously entering that inky morose,
      they reach out to touch as they shake in their shoes.
Two littlest cherubs are on duty there too,
      there just to support and enable, not do.

So they mostly stay out of everyone's way.
      The women, aware of a mysterious Presence,
unworldly, furtive; what is that faint essence?
      Just how to explain it escapes common senses.

One thing for sure, the women would swear.
      (Their work hadn't even commenced back in there.)
It's mysterious, ghostly and scary, they fear.
      But the only thing certain is: He is not here!

God's two littlest angels take care to stay mum,
      to shut up and be quiet, just twiddle their thumbs.
Not easy for two little cherubs, you see,
      but so they were ordered and so it shall be.

They are watchful, obedient yet still unobtrusive
      as the women approach, scared half to death.
Not a feather there twitched, not a sigh was there heard.
      By all mortal standards no message inferred.

Yet somehow those women feel something amiss.
      They freeze in their steps to see what's coming next.

In the Sweet Gum Tree

No one knows how they could sense that Presence,
    and the women themselves are not making much sense.

But they "saw a young man" who gave them instructions
    on what to report to their brother disciples.
No matter whatever instructions were given
    there was no follow-up on the letter or sense of them.

But Ralphie and Ailie are hot to contribute.
    They confer with each other off to the side.
"Our orders are focused on non-interference
    with initiatives taken by mortals encountered,

"with a notable lack of specific instructions
    on initiatives we conger up on our own."
It was Ailie first spotted this clear opportunity.
    She yanked Ralphie's wing and brashly observed:

"There's a chance here before us to scoop this whole story.
    The spirit controlling the program thus far
is death, condemnation, dark tombs and the blues.
    And that is quite clearly nobody's Good News.

"Now spirit is something within our domain.
    So, let's grab on, take hold and make it our claim.
What we need instead of gloom, doom and the blues
    are lilies and eggs, bowties and red shoes,

"babe chicks and small bunnies for kids to enjoy.
    The new spirit we need must this theme employ:
New life everywhere! New life celebration.
    New life for all and it's called Resurrection."

Ralphie caught on to her insight immediately.
    No need to draw pictures for him.
They donned pretty clothing of colorful hues,
    reds, greens and yellows with ribbons of blues.

They colored some eggs for their bird-nest like baskets
　　　then hid them around as wild critters might do.
With this they were set for a first annual test,
　　　except that they hadn't named that first day yet.

"Resurrection Celebration is far, far too cumbersome.
　　　Something shorter and merrier is desired, required.
Empty Tomb Day congers images of doom.
　　　We must find a theme more like *Flowers in June."*

Once more it was Ailie, her eye on the target
　　　as she shouted, "Eureka, I think that I've got it!
A name that just naturally connects with new bonnets
　　　and flowers, dyed eggs and bright airy sonnets.

*"Easter'*s the name of the day we shall hallow,
　　　as the day we shout praise and give thanks for New Life.
The name connects up with all themes of the day
　　　as in egg and parade, as in bowties and bonnets!"

But Satan did not overlook these advances.
　　　He could see the destructive potential they posed.
If humans would celebrate this day forever,
　　　his case was doomed and his cause served, never.

Thus, it came to be that God's two littlest angels
　　　were Satan's gravest opponents on earth.
Satan must find ways to thwart their influence here
　　　or his plans for humans in hell disappear.

Gabriel intervened on behalf of his cherubs.
　　　The case went to Heaven's highest high court.
The Justices deliberated six days and six nights.
　　　The result: A New Act of Creation, by rights.

Gabriel read the verdict in deep sonorous tones.
    "Not only is Easter a Grand annual Feast Day
but every first day in the week, come what may,
    is now Easter too, a high holy feast day."

MY *THOUGHTS* ARE WITH YOU?

When a friend is in trouble or suffering pain
    we remember that friend in our prayer once again.
Then over and over, the name is recalled
    and we pray once again that the pain be resolved.

And so it seems natural to pray without ceasing
    for all those we know whose pain should be decreasing.
But apologetic we needn't feel, ever
    for seeking God's help for those under the weather.

And yet it seems fashionable now and again
    to avoid words like *prayer* or *god bless* or *amen.*
Instead we send *wishes* or *thoughts,* even *greetings.*
    Then silently pray that our friend is a'healing.

But why such avoidance and mindless behavior?
    Blurt it right out; let the world hear our shout.
We beg for God's healing, that's what it's about.
    No puttsying around, no reason to doubt.

So I'm here to tell you, no fooling around
    I'm steady at prayer that your health soon rebound.
I pray that God's blessing, his grace and his peace
    enfold you in love that will never surcease.

While doctors and nurses are doing their part
  we'll pray for a boost from the Lord at the start.
And too, for all those in the healing profession,
  prayers of petition, thanksgiving, confession.

Don't send me your thoughts or your cares or your wishes
  when I'm in pain or suffering with twitches.
Tell me up front you pray my health's restored.
  Let the world know we both count on the Lord!

Acts 16:16-24

THE SEER

She was a youngster of about eight at the time,
    picked up by some troops on a raid near the Rhine,
now bound for the foreign slave market in Rome
    never again to see family or home.

A grizzled old merchant fed up with kibitzin'
    purchased the girl for some help in his kitchen.
She quickly caught on and soon won his wife's favor
    with upbeat demeanor and graceful behavior.

Her mistress soon learned of her wisdom with dreams,
    of her reading of palms and star signs and such things.
She analyzed patterns for well-to-do clients,
    happy to pay for her trusted reliance.

A valued resource in that part of the town,
    well known by the merchants and folk hanging 'round
as an effective clairvoyant to believe in or fear
    and they called her Belinda Lea the Seer.

She just chanced to be out and about on the block
    when Paul and friend Silas (about two o'clock)
showed up and commenced to look over the city.
    With Paul in particular, she felt this affinity.

Such a mystical cast to his public demeanor,
    something about him allayed all her fear.
Compelled to stick by these two out-of-town men
    she grasped all at once Paul's preaching to them.

Then to Paul's annoyance this waif soon began
   her own sidewalk preaching right there and just then.
She knew how to get hold of her audience's attention.
   "Hey, listen to these guys, they're prophets worth mention.

"Listen up, they can tell you how you can be saved."
   Paul soon had his fill so he went to the kid
and commanded the spirit that crazed her, "Get out!
   I command you to leave her, quit now, and out!"

The poor girl was shaken, no longer possessed.
   Her worth as a seer had been put to rest.
Belinda, of no further use to her mistress,
   was just booted out, one small urban distress.

No family or lodging and nothing to do,
   no school and no teachers, seemingly through.
She just tailed along with Paul and with Silas
   but now, somewhat wiser, she maintained her silence.

It didn't take long for this street-wisened urchin
   to learn that her heroes were perfectly able
to trigger a ruckus wherever they went
   and they didn't need her to get all out of bent.

A couple of bullies were watching those two,
   there to protect their home 'hood from intruders.
Silas and Paul, clearly out-of-town men
   so they started a street fight with them there and then.

Alarm soon was sent of a neighborhood brawl.
   Police quickly responded, a nine-one-one call.
Not exactly a SWAT team but ample in count
   to intimidate all who were out and about.

In the Sweet Gum Tree

The cops, more concerned about quiet than justice
	beat the tar out of both Paul and friend Silas.
Then when black and blue, threw them into the clink
	to give them, they said, some down-time to think.

Belinda, alone now and nowhere to go,
	hung out near the jail just tracking the show.
It was quiet and peaceful on into that evening
	after the din of the day just preceding.

The prisoners by now settled down for a snooze.
	The guards "on alert," were sharing some booze.
Along about midnight, Belinda awakened
	to sounds of camp singing and minor earth-shaking.

Prisoners and guards in rich harmony singing,
	praising the Lord with a guitar a'plinking.
We could hear distinctly *Kumbyah* and some more,
	and a Roman rendition of *Row us Ashore*.

Very peaceful indeed 'gainst the fuss of the day,
	so many voices praising God's way.
But a guard rushed right in; it made no sense to him
	(given their way with prisoners), those voices within.

The sentry discovered their chains in a pile;
	inmates free as birds harmonized all the while.
Then once again a quake trembled the ground,
	and busted gate hinges throughout the compound.

With that all the prisoners sang bolder and louder.
	Belinda had also been tailing the jailer
right into the dirty, dank, dark, dreadful prison,
	a curious kid on one dim, futile mission.

The guard grabbed his knife to take his own life
      when Paul talked the man out of that notion.
"See we are all here, no one has escaped,
      no need for your dying midst all this commotion."

He fell on his knees groveling and shaking,
      "Sir, what must we do to share that life with you?"
Paul told him the Good News of Jesus the Savior
      and they all retired to the jailer's own station.

The newcomers, baptized in a fountain outside
      at the jailer's home quarters right there where they met.
Then he put on a feast no one will forget.
      The gossip still echoes o'er that party yet.

The reveling went on all through that long night,
      till the far eastern sky became tinted with light.
The morning saw Paul and friend Silas all ready
      for an early departure continuing their travel.

Belinda Lea had slept over that night
      as a guest of the jailer's own youngsters.
For a kid of just eight she had seen a wild time
      since abducted by soldiers up north on the Rhine.

Once more, she had never lost track of her gifts
      since Paul's exorcise on the pathway in Rome.
But no need to have Paul as an antagonist
      if she could cool it and have him instead as a friend.

So she laid low for now and went with the flow,
      biding her time while pondering Paul's tales.
The Good News he preached sunk in and took root
      and she had become a street preacher to boot.

Scarce closer to nine now, a crush on the guard's lad,
    she just settled in and made his place her new pad.
With zeal for the Lord and Paul's slant on dogmatics
    the extended family had their own polemics.

That little church flourished through years and then centuries,
    through tumults and wars, laughter and tears;
through destruction, restructuring, and budget arears,
    dedications and blessings, christenings and fears.

It is well known today as St. Peter's of Rome,
    a holy cathedral of stained glass and stone.
A center of Sacrament and God's Holy Word
    that all the world's faithful may think of as home.

A side chapel still shines all through that ancient history,
    dedicated to strays of migrations and nations.
The gold-sterling plates on the gate of the nave state:
    To Belinda Lea, Patron Saint
of all of the World's Tiniest Wandering Waifs.

RESCUE US

Hear now our plea, oh our shepherd and leader,
    you who reign over the realms of the angels.
Right here in the face of all peoples and tribes
    amass your great strength; come save our bruised hides.

    "Redeem us, oh Lord," is our lasting song.
    In your glory return us to where we belong.

Oh Lord God of hosts, how long will you anger
    in spite of our multiple, fraught supplications?
The daily bread you have spread on our way
    is the deep briny draft of our own tears we drink.
Because of you all the nations deride us,
    we are but a joke and seem destined to sink.

    "Redeem us, oh Lord," is our lasting song.
    In your glory return us to where we belong.

You brought us up out of our bondage in Egypt.
    Like kudzu we up and took over the land.
The mountains were lost in our colossal shadow,
    the towering trees in our lofty boughs.
You stretched out our fronds to the ocean's far shores;
    our branches extended up and over the clouds.

Now our fences are flattened, our walls broken down.
    Transients are stuffing themselves with our grapes.
Wild pigs are uprooting the vines as they please.
    The elk and the deer graze our meadows at ease.
Lord, God of hosts, look after your vineyard.
    Preserve with your left what your right hand has planted.

Those who have wreaked all this havoc upon us?
    Consume them right now in your blistering glance.
Then take by the hand the babe that you sired,
    this child you have brought to adulthood.
We will never, forever fail you again.
    Fill our lungs with your life; we will shout out your name.

    "Redeem us, oh Lord," is our lasting song.
    In your glory return us to where we belong.

A Red-shouldered Hawk

Isaiah 61:1-4; 8-11

RIGHTEOUSNESS IN BLOOM

The spirit of God is upon me.
He has anointed me and he has sent me
to preach the good news to all the oppressed,
to revive the broken in spirit.
To proclaim freedom, release to all prisoners,
to pardon all those already convicted.

To announce the year of the Lord's grace:
a day of celebration of our God's victory
and relief for the comfort all those who grieve.
To provide for those who mourn:
with garlands of roses instead of more ashes,
the oil of gladness instead of more sadness and
a mantle of praise to recharge weakened spirits.

They will be called, "oaks of righteousness"
planted by God to show off his glory.
They will restore the ancient carcasses,
rebuild all that old worn out rubble.

Think of it: the original *Urban Renewal Project*;
a New City in place of that tired old slum.
Up from the wreckage of generations, to a
transformed commune of my own disciples.

For I, the Lord, love justice.
I hate robbery and all kinds of transgression.
I will faithfully give them their restoration
and with them will create an eternal covenant.

Their descendants will be known among nations,
    their offspring renowned everywhere
    and all who see them will sense
    they are the people the Lord God has blessed.

I will greatly rejoice in the Lord,
    my whole being revel in God.
For he has dressed me in clothes of salvation
    with the mantle of righteousness.
    Like a bridegroom in tuxedo struts in with poise
    and a bride proudly shows off all her jewelry,

so, too, the earth brings forth what it sprouts
    and a garden makes what is sown in it spring up
    and so will the Lord cause justice and praise
    to spring up and explode into blossom
    right here and now and before all the nations.

PAUL'S FAILURE

So, this is their bragged about, colossal Athens,
  a junkyard of images, altars and ravings
and citizens sick with idolatrous cravings.
  A metropolis awash in its pagan engravings.

Paul mixed it up, strolled around as he listened.
  He got some attention as they listened too.
"Interest in doctrine," was their dire affliction,
  leaders that curious, yet so irreligious.

Confessing beliefs in weird, strange-sounding faiths
  with ardor and passion, so eager to bait.
Pure head-trips however, no heart or soul in it,
  theory, reflection, all talk, no conviction.

Curious about Paul's unique take on these matters,
  eager for more of his novel, foreign chatter.
Learned philosophers attacked him head on,
  gossip and rumors, tall tales till the dawn.

Paul's teaching on their ears – no doubt about it –
  as weird as their inane notions on his.
Yet, not taken lightly, these prime, ancient sages;
  philosophy's profited a lot through the ages.

Respect for those roots gave Paul cause for caution.
  But somehow *this* Athens did not fit the mold.
So, a "yes" nod to caution, but "no" to duplicity
  for Paul was as learned as any in this fold.

In the Sweet Gum Tree

So they went to the forum to talk it all through
     and Paul took his place to make his case anew.
While the doctors of Athens gave him his due
     in pondering his concepts and his point of view.

Paul stood at the lectern addressing them all,
     "Athenians, I see how religious you are.
As I toured your fair city I saw this inscription,
     'To an unknown god,' as an altar description.

"This mysterious god now to you an unknown
     is the very same God that is yours for your own.
The God who created all we'll ever know
     is Lord of all heaven and earth here below.

"He lives not in shrines made by our calloused hands
     and is not served by human catering fans
as though he were poor or in need of assistance
     since he is the one who gives our existence.

"Yes, it is he provides all of us our daily rations,
     who has given us places with boundaries as nations,
allotted us times of existence and being
     and indeed is as close as our very own breathing.

"For in him we live, move, indeed have our being
     as some of your poets in their time have said:
'We are God created,' to quote them exactly
     and if that is so, it is not ipso facto

to think that some artist with hammer and chisel
     could craft us a god out of marble or pixel.
God's not the creative product of sculptors
     at work in their factory or smelters or foundries.

211

"In our age of ignorance and innocent bliss
        God quickly forgave this disgracefulness.
But now times are different. New messages sent
        and all people today are called to repent.

"We have since received a life-changing disclosure.
        The day has been set to get our act together.
The judge is now known in this new revelation;
        it's God-guaranteed in our Lord's resurrection."

But Athenians were still not converted that day.
        Their idols and toys of gold, silver and clay
remained their prime objects of reverent devotion,
        the vain, stupid source of their childish emotion.

Grave interest in doctrine was there all around
        but zeal for the Lord was nowhere to be found.
Paul botched his one chance, his mission ground down
        and he failed to found a new church in that town!

SACRAMENTAL

Materialism is commonly scorned
    as vilely capitalistic,
while Spiritualism is often preferred
    by the Mystical-Opportunistic.
Such assessments come free but I'm sure you agree
are not in the least realistic.

Spiritualism is not our top value
    nor materialism rejected.
For there is in addition this minor point
to be here and for now at least, recollected:
    of all the world's sinning
most is attributable to influences
generally perceived to be spiritual.

Hatred and greed, envy and lust
    flow copiously from our spiritual seeds.
See, all are contributors
    to negative deeds
and none are among
appetites we should feed.

Love, peace and joy
    are all spiritual sources.
And they do find expression in high moral choices.
    But, spirituality is never determinative
on whether an action
is morally affirmative.

Spirituality's uncritically praised,
      acclaimed with far too much credit.
Materialism gets too much bad press,
      while material items by God's Word are blessed.

Could it be we are into a total reverse
on which is the better, which is the worse?

By combining the pair we get something new,
      not there when we viewed the original two.
Spirit through matter is deemed sacramental,
      so sacrament's the newly discovered reality.
Thus, spiritual/material is not the whole range
for expressing of moods or the stressing of sage.

This is the much better solution available
      than one or the both of those on the table.
Sacrament's surely the best of the lot.
      The root of it's spiritual, the stuff of it's not.
Combining the spiritual intentionality
with substance entirely physically stable,

an outward and visible element signing
      an inward and spiritual blessing aligning.
The gift of both realms' graces abounding
      enriching us all in procedures astounding.
Because God determined by his plan so clever,
that we should delight in his blessings forever.

1 Kings 19:9-18

A WORD OF SILENCE

Elijah hid out in a cave on Mount Horeb.
    The Lord chased him down even there.
"What in the world do you think you are up to,
    pawing around in the ground like some bear?"

"I'm the only one left," Elijah complained,
    "Your prophets are dead, your altars thrown down.
They all have forsaken your sanctified covenant.
    Now I am the target of hatred unbound."

Then came this great windstorm reverberating,
    so fierce it was tearing up mountains.
It shattered the rocks into slivers and bits,
    but no word was heard in the tempest.

Then a great fire a'blazing and roaring
    but no word was heard in that ferocious inferno.
Then this wild earthquake came splitting the ground
    but there in the earthquake, no spoken sound.

Then softly a Word in the midst of sheer silence.
    He wrapped up his face in his mantle.
Elijah stepped cautiously outside the cave,
    now ready to hear and to follow.

"Quit playing the victim! You haven't been duped.
    I have many thousands still not in that crowd,
knees still not bent and lips never pursed.
    Recall that my Word doesn't need to be loud."

215

HANDPRINT ON THE GLASS

When the morning dew is new on the pane
      of the sliding glass door to the east,
and the rising sun sets a gem in each drop
      of the mist that's adorning that morning feast,
a handprint appears in the film on that glass
      provoking a smile and sometimes a tear,
so delicate, so small, so petit and refined
      and I know that of course it sure isn't mine.

The print is not clear as a single impression,
      but overlaid frequently, you could say habitually
by a regular passer through this route and door.
      The fingers point up from this moisty small palm,
not as in a start but as brace-keeping-balance
      in a graceful pirouette in departing my space
and I'm left with the print in the dew on my door
      but no trace of the passing on ceiling or floor.

Come Friday that multiple print will be gone.
      Friday's the day for the housekeeper's call.
The place will be laundered, scrubbed down, dusted clean,
      end to end, shelf and sill, outside, in between.
Dust must never settle, handprints are verboten;
      new standards in place under her watchful eye.
Glass will be wiped down one side at a time
      then thoroughly cleaned of all prints, hers and mine.

That lovely handprint will be gone from the door,
  but no need to fret, it'll be back as before.
For the palm that left that print on the pane
  will pass through again in her grace just the same.
She'll gladden my heart and brighten my day
  enliven my mood as in fresh morning dew.
The slate will be clear for impressing new tracks
  in the dew that appears there each morn on the glass.

SEVENTY TIMES SEVEN

I know that our standard's forgiveness.
        But Lord, just how far must I go?
If some member persistently dishes up crud
        should I offer my cheek seven times to that thug?

You are missing the point, there is no limit set,
        no keeping track and no looking back.
You're surely no judge and hardly a jury
        but take timely note of this kingdom story:

There once was a master out settling accounts
        with members of his household staff.
By turn he reviewed each servant's amount
        and settled those tallies account by account.

The first on the seat was this noted deadbeat.
        His debt was way over his head,
so far in the red he could never see black;
        no point to be gained in persisting with that.

The master could see nothing other to do
        than to eat the bad debt (Well, wouldn't you?),
then pitch this free loader right out on the street.
        About time for that nit to stand up on his feet.

But the servant, you see, then fell down on his knees.
        "Have patience my master, oh please," pleaded he.
He groveled, implored and prayed on his knee,
        "With time I'll get all of it paid," beseeched he.

In the Sweet Gum Tree

With tears in his eyes and voice all a'quiver,
    he clung to his master in deep supplication.
The master was touched to the quick and repented.
    He wrote off the whole of that debt obligation.

The servant was free now and clear of his debt,
    an albatross dropped from his wretched neck.
Certainly not by his worth or word,
    but a merciful act of his master and lord.

Now clear of that judgment crisis, the fool
    pulled up his socks and returned to his vices.
Word got around he'd avoided disaster
    in settling accounts with their common master.

Another slave then approaching the first
    put this timely wish on his "to do" list:
"Hey mate, ain't it great, that sweet deal you rate
    in settling the balance on your real estate?

Now could you, my brother, give me extra time
    for satisfying that little debit of mine
incurred over lunch at last Saturday's game
    when I was flat broke, not a dime to my name?"

But that slave insisted this fellow pay up,
    no matter his kid needed braces.
He bullied and threatened; the poor guy rescinded
    and paid that lunch debit completely.

There were too many witnesses there and around
    to that servant's stand on that matter at hand.
And needless to say, the word made its way
    unerringly back to the master's own bay.

A Red-shouldered Hawk

The wicked deadbeat was trapped then and there
        and called back to appear on the carpet.
The master confronted, now stern and some wiser.
            The slave crossed his legs and squeezed his thighs tighter.

"I forgave you much more than you ever were worth.
            Why couldn't you do less for your brother?
I'm rescinding my judgment. You now go to prison
            where you'll spend the balance of your worthless life."

The Lord then returned to the question before them:
            Seven? Oh my no, you've missed the whole meaning.
It's not just a matter of times or occasions;
            but, *seventy times seven* might give you some feeling.

There shall be no holding back in forgiveness.
            And the fate of that no-account servant recounted
is your fate indeed if you fail to forgive
            as by God you're already forgiven.

A TELEOLOGICAL OPTION

Who made up the rule that purpose comes first
and determines the plan of the action?
Why not see initially the action kick-off,
then purpose can find its place after?

A cause is assumed to precede the effect
and create the effect's unique traits.
Why can't we see first the result and its specs
then up and create an acceptable launcher?

Results, we are told, can't be first on the scene;
there must first be a triggering reason.
Why not just approve the result in advance
and then fabricate a responsible trigger?

Why couldn't there be a signal out front
compelling us all toward bold, daring action?
Without detailing outcomes and results
or even recounting each minute infraction?

Who said that the ends must justify means?
That sequence is sure not divine.
Let's challenge that order at least this one time.
Choose means that delight, results might be fine!

UNGRATEFUL BELOVED

I planted a fine vineyard on a very fertile hill.
　I cleared the ground of stones and added there a still.
I hoed, I raked, I pulled out weeds.
I tilled around those creepers' leads.
　I thinned the growth and pruned the vines
to stimulate their growing needs.

I built a watchtower on a grade on center in my garden,
　set out the best varieties for that side of the mountain.
Yet all that I got from all of that was wild and bitter fruit.
　Now, you be judge of me and mine and my futile pursuit.

What more, I pray, could I have done in all my careful farmin'
　to guarantee that I would have a rich, productive garden?
I'll tell you what I am going to do, tear down the wall around it,
　remove all that stone and cut out the hedge that surrounds it.

With no irrigation, no planter's attention,
　and no protection from thieves' intervention,
with no one around to prevent their crude rooting
the wild boars will soon make it a mud hole for wallowing.
　Then will we see without ever blinking
a tangle of weeds trampled and mangled, abandoned and stinking.

For the vineyard in question is you, oh my people.
　In you I invested my greatest and best
and from you expected justice and righteousness.
But I get bloodshed and cries and wails of despair,
　no feel of achievement, no sense of success
and no fruit for me from my garden.

Romans 8:22-27

PREGNANCY

The whole pregnant creation, including us too,
    has been groaning in birth pangs and pain.
We carry first fruits of the Spirit of God
    and our bodies cry out for deliverance soon.

For in hope we were saved and as everyone knows,
    what is hoped for is never in sight.
Who hopes for an item already in view?
    So, we hope, we await and in patience endure.

What's growing within us is not getting smaller
    and of course we can't see it as yet.
But the longer we wait the larger it gets
    and the joy in our anticipation still grows.

So we pray with no words on our lips
    while the Spirit speaks on our behalf.
We've no words to say it but Spirit to pray it
    with sighs far too deep for our quiet wish.

With God searching our very heart rhythms
    informed by the mind of the Spirit,
the prayer of the Spirit is on our behalf
    and precisely in sync with the notions of God.

TIME
Durations and Trends

It can easily be reckoned in centuries or seconds,
     eons or eras, days, months or years.
Yet fastidious computing defies comprehension.
     I have no idea of just *what* they are doing.

Even worse, more remorse is this sad admission,
     I haven't the foggiest notion
of just what *IT* is that's so easily reckoned
     yet no one I find can define with precision?

While time is that mystery no one can define,
     there's no mystery to it 'till I try to do it.
Everyone knows what's a second or season
     but what is that lapse that occurs in between them?

Seconds and hours count out our endurance
     as inches and miles note spaces and distance.
When all's said and done I still have no clue
     as to what's been endured when enduring is through.

Yardsticks and clocks just don't talk to each other.
     Inches and minutes have no common rhythms.
Explaining endurance in terms of expanse?
     Try using truck fenders to hold up your pants.

Why time was initially thought up and invented . . .
     Eureka, you know? I think I might have it!
To serve as a vault to store all of our stories,
     access to that crypt then restricted to memories.

In the Sweet Gum Tree

Stories in time-vaults or crypts are superior
    to reproduced copies in book-hoards and side-boards.
Stories live on with quick pulses and breathing
    untouched by damp dust and fictitious believing.

But that little side-step does not solve our riddle.
    The query addressed there was *Why,* not *What is it?*
What is it remains in mysterious gaps
    in the vacuum enduring through all that time lapse.

I've done it again, assumed time's reality
    in my unthinking reference to a vacuous time lapse,
when I know of no way a gap could have ensued
    in the lapse of a span in a finite time gasp.

The speed of light squared could be the lost chord
    in our medley of added, finite, causal factors.
Times that by M and that brings us to E,
    but time and endurance still seem to elude us.

Length times the width will achieve broader views,
    times that by the height to get deeper intuit.
All that times the time to arrive at reality,
    a fantastic, pentagonal, unsketchable, quantality.

That's as far as I go. Time remains an enigma.
    We keep losing track of it. Where does it all go?
Experience and birthdays add up every year
    and the years roll relentlessly on, as you know.

I should be far wiser today than back then,
    but I don't have the time to decipher time's bend.
While I doubt that the story extends past its end,
    I've noticed that *IT* is not showing a trend.

225

SOUND
Harmonic and Discordant Mysteries

There's a mystery called sound: elusive, profound,
      we can't see, smell or feel, yet near always around.
It can please us or tease us, scare or deceive us,
      be beautiful, spiritual, glorious or grand.

It can also be squeaky, nerve-wracking and shrill,
      prompt wonder and awe, a devotional thrill.
But exactly what is it? I haven't a clue.
      As old as the hills and yet always brand new.

Sound as we know it begins in some thing
      such as drum, bell or horn or a vibrating string.
It then needs a medium to transport the vibes
      such as water or air or some other conductor.

The final essential's a conscious receptor
      commonly known as an ear that can hear.
So, source, conductor and sentient receiver
      are required components for this mystery's believer.

Absent a source or vibrating beginning
      creation is silent, no crying, no singing.
Vibes in a vacuum have nowhere to go.
      In fact, they can't even be in there for show.

Vibes could resonate with some fork or a string
      but no ear to catch meaning, it just doesn't ring!
Does a tree make a sound when it falls to the ground
      with no ear even near there to hear it come down?

In the Sweet Gum Tree

A mighty red oak tree stood tall in the wood
        for a hundred and twenty five winters.
Still in its prime it succumbed to a storm as
        the lightening exploded its trunk into splinters.

The tree crumbled down to the damp forest floor
        but there was, shall we say, not a witness,
no critter, no human, no sentient being.
        So, the forest was silent midst that entire tempest.

Yet, if you had been there both quiet and blind,
        your head would have been dinging and ringing
with stereophonic vibrations a'mingling
        and maybe – who knows? – with harmonious singing.

REVERIE

Her head rests deep in my shoulder.
     My arm enfolds about her.
I feel the soft warmth of her presence
     as cheek upon cheek we embrace
while wisps of her hair drift in the air
     seeking permission to tickle my face.

I pull her in close to assure I don't lose her.
     She snuggles up nearer, agreeing.
We shift our weight slightly
     right here where we're sitting
comfortably entwined on the chair,
     like it's all meant to be and so very fitting.

As I awaken from out of my slumber
     it's, "only a dream" I'm reminded again!
But in dream and rich memory I'm once more with her
     and in that sweet theme I am blessed as before!
Yet for that brief moment it was real for me.
     Skip it for now and just let me be!

In the Sweet Gum Tree

Psalm 104:24-35

SING PRAISES

What an awesome, spectacular world you have made
    with Wisdom, your partner at your right hand.
You've created the earth with its myriads of creatures,
    the sea, vast and deep, its mind-boggling features,
    with schools of fish beyond our mental reaches.

See, there's your pet dragon created for kicks
    romping and playing and fetching your sticks.
You feed and sustain; without you they are nothing,
    while out of your view even cease from existing.

It's in your vitality they blossom and grow.
    Without it they're fragments and finally blow.
See our tiny ships there a'bobbing and drifting,
    such puny additions to all that existing.

May the glory of God live on now forever
    and may you, O Lord, enjoy creating always.
You look on the earth and see how it trembles,
    reach out to a mountain and Alas– it explodes.

I will sing to my God as long as I breathe
I will praise him forever and ever.

May my song please you my Lord and my God,
    as it gives me much pleasure in singing.
        Bless the Lord O my soul. Hallelujah!

A Red-shouldered Hawk

BIBLICAL INDEX

Page

In the Sweet Gum Tree

Mark 9:2-9	132
Mark 12:29-31	31
Mark 13:24-27	194
Mark 15 – 16:8	195
Mark 16:1-8	10
Luke 2:25-35	48
Luke 7	34
Luke 10:38-42	113
Luke 12:15-21	108
Luke 15:11-32	19
John 1:1-18	1
John 5:1-14	29
John 11	113
John 19:30	152
Acts 2:1-42	86
Acts 2:42	127
Acts 9:10-19	67
Acts 9:32-43	43
Acts 16:16-24	201
Acts 17:16-31	210
Romans 7	122
Romans 7:7ff	181
Romans 8:22-27	223
Romans 14:1-12	178
I Corinthians 12:27-14:1	96
Philippians 3:4-14	192
Philippians 4:4-8	172
Hebrews 11:1-12:3	145
James 1:11-18	103
Revelation 21	153

BIOGRAPHICAL NOTES

Page

17   **Lloyd Gressle** and I were close friends for many years. At the time of writing this piece, he was bishop of the Diocese of Bethlehem and I was under contract with the diocese for services regarding planning and personnel. "**Marg**" was his wife. Fred was **Fred Wernickie**, Lloyd's predecessor. Others mentioned were members of the diocesan staff in Bethlehem.

35   **Charlene** is my daughter, also an author and currently publisher of my printed material. The rings prompting this ditty were crafted out of material from a fallen star.

52   **Lynne** was my wife, colleague and partner in church work. She died in January, 2006, leaving a huge blank in my life. For no particular reason that I can think of, I was moved some six years later to meditate once again on our journey together. *PRESENCE* came out of that experience

55   **Wesley Frensdorff** was a very close colleague, friend and fellow champion in the cause of promoting Baptismal Ministry. He was Bishop of Nevada 1972-1985. I don't remember what excuse I had for penning this limerick or even when I did it, but Wes was an incurable punster and deserved it. He was killed in the crash of a small plane in the Grand Canyon in 1988. In 1990 Lynne and I published a collection of essays in his memory called *RESHAPING MINISTRY (Jethro Publ.)*

59   **Lynne** and I were supporters of Cursillo but not of the too-syrupy piety that sometimes found expression in the movement. That's apparent in this sample of *palanca*.

125 **St. John Chrysostom** A church in a west Denver suburb I
served as Interim Rector and Rector Search Consultant for a while in
the 80s. I was invited many years later to write something for a scrap-
book they were assembling for the observance of some anniversary.

139 **Deborah** is my middle daughter. When she was a ten or
twelve year old a box turtle showed up in our back yard. The kids
played around with him for a couple days. While our back-yard fence
would restrain the dog, it was not turtle proof and we didn't want to
see our new "pet" get out on the street. So we took him to a park
nearby and released him on the bank of a small stream. It was during
his brief sojourn with us that Deb, examining him one day in a playful,
curious and mildly frustrated mood asked, of no one in particular,
"Well, how do you pet a turtle?"

A Red-shouldered Hawk